Unheard Voices

By Liz Otterbein RN

Journal of a Psychiatric Nurse
27,533 Words
2016

Names have been changed to protect the privacy of individuals.

Contents

Acknowledgements

To late Tony Perry who trusted my writing.

Thank you to Johan Wassenaar for encouraging me to write this book and for his caring coaching through the process. Thanks to my mother-in-law, Jackie Otterbein and Doug Adrianson for graciously editing the book.

Thank you Chris Brennan for the Art work on the cover, and Nina Mecagni for designing it.

This book would not exist without my friends, Chris, Olivia, Karunya, Leslie, Meribeth, Anat, Arthur, Felix, Gopal, Sunsoung, Em, Greg, Carol, Gil, Jeremy, Françoise, Leslie, Philippe, Laurie, Michael and of course the huge support of my family Jeff, Jen, Joel and my dear ones in France.

I want to thank the nurses and doctors I worked with for 14 years, my dear supervisor Sandy for showing me the way and of course Linda, Lynn and Buck for being with me on that December 4th.

Introduction

I spent 14 years of my life working in a psychiatric hospital. Often, after my 12-hour shift, I would journal about a patient who had attracted my attention or touched my heart that day. My first intention was really to clear my soul—writing can do that. Reading those stories again now, I see the importance of shining a light on a world so often misjudged.

Our unit was a short-term facility, meaning that most people were on a three-day legal hold, called a 5150. A "qualified" person can determine that one needs an evaluation against their will for any of three reasons: danger to self, danger to others, or gravely disabled for psychological reasons.

In our psychiatric world we have a lot of diagnoses, all neatly organized with codes in our bible: the *Diagnostic and Statistical Manual of Mental Disorders (DSM 5)*. Educated knowledge is important in many ways, but I still believe at times it is possible to keep our academic learning in abeyance and take a totally different approach—an approach that comes from listening deeply, without trying to analyze, label, or even to help. An approach that comes from a genuine interest, along the lines of: "I am not in your shoes, please tell me about yourself."

When I first began working in this acute locked facility, I saw staff members take one look at a new arrival and have an immediate visible reaction which I could not always understand. They may spot a small red scarf around the neck and assume that they were being confronted by a gang member. To me, having come from a nursing job in a geriatric psychiatric hospital in Switzerland, all I saw was a young man shackled at his ankles and wrists and I just wondered about the road that brought him there. That is what I meant about knowledge interfering with seeing.

Maybe I learned the stickiness of labels, diagnoses, and all the recommendations that go with them, when I was really young. Early on I was told: "You are dyslexic." "You are not academic; maybe wood shop is your best choice." "You are an artist; you should be a sculptor." These labels were not helpful.

Thinking we know what is best for someone, approaching another with a solution picked from some book, is not the way I want to be with people. I want to keep my curiosity alive. Maybe the simple act of looking together without coming from the known, will allow something else to happen.

After a violent assault on our unit injured three nurses, me included, I was suddenly faced with my own deep fear. To my surprise I went right into advice and self-judgment. It took me more than two years to understand that the same deep compassionate listening that I was giving to my patients, I could give to myself. When I accepted my fears and sadness without judgment, without trying to fix them, my brain and my heart started to heal.

This book is in no way a complete view of the psychiatric world, it is a journal and my journey.

***

Rachelle: Fear beneath anger

"Code Grey" was called several times from the Crisis Team Unit, indicating an urgent need for backup due to a combative person. Several of us ran to the wing of the hospital that was asking for help. When we opened the double doors that separated our unit from theirs, we saw a short female staff member backed up against the wall and a tall thin woman yelling and verbally threatening her, using extremely foul language.

After so many years inside these walls, insults sometimes glide over me and I don't really hear them anymore, so it is difficult after the fact to really remember them. Clear in my memory was that I was focused on watching and reading the body language of this young woman. I was watching the tension in her hands and fists and paying attention to my own body reactions.

She was very close to a small Latina staff member, insulting her and posturing threats with her upper chest, her arms held still along her thin body.

Because we arrived from the back and she was busy yelling, Eric, one of the RNs, slid his hands from her shoulder down to her arms in a strong but gentle way, closing his hands on both her wrists. She did not fight to get out of the grip and turned quickly towards the person who was touching her. Her face stopped halfway when her eyes landed on mine.

I did not tell her what to do or not to do, I only shared my most important concern at the time: safety, physical safety. I heard myself saying "We are only concerned with safety. Please come with me." From my training I knew that in full anger the person can only hear very short sentences. I was told no more than five words per sentence.

So I repeated in a tone slightly lower than hers: "We are only concerned with safety" and I asked her to follow me into the unit. To my surprise, she complied right away and walked without any physical prompting. The psychological pressure of all the staff around certainly helped her make that decision.

With all the staff still around her, I told her that nobody would hurt her. She immediately came closer to me.

For my comfort and because of our training, I usually kept a safe distance from a patient in that state of rage. Our training recommends two arm lengths. This time I showed no resistance to her approach.

She turned her head away from me and yelled one more insult at the female staff member still standing there. She got so close to me that I felt her shoulder against mine as we started to walk toward our unit. Eric was walking right behind us; he had let go of her arms but was ready to move in if necessary.

In short sentences I continued to repeat my concern with safety, hers and ours, my voice getting progressively softer.

We passed the double doors to our unit like conjoined twins hooked at the shoulders. I asked her to sit on the bed of the first seclusion room and I felt compelled to sit next to her. At that point she decided to rest her head on my shoulder and it was natural for me to put my arm around her and start rocking her.

In a matter of minutes this agitated, threatening young woman went from yelling to rocking in my arms. I was not sure what was happening. I could hear myself repeating, "Nobody is going to hurt you; you are safe here."

Everybody left and I stayed with her for a while and she started to talk. It was not a surprise to hear of her long history of abuse. It was probably one of the worst stories I had ever heard. Writing about her that night I noticed that my pen, my hand and my heart did not want to print it on paper, wishing that one day I would forget it.

Later that day a nurse who I respect asked me, "How do you do that?"

"Do what?" I asked.

"What you did with Rachelle."

I was at a loss for words to answer her, but her question helped me to reflect on my work. Are we so trained in our responses that we cannot see beneath anger the fear and the suffering in others? I saw Rachelle as a human being in pain and this guided my response.

* * *

Margaret: Extreme spiritual quest

Margaret was admitted to our unit after wandering the streets with no clothes on. I guess that is what made her fall into the category of "danger to self," so she was put on a three-day legal hold.

Without resistance on her part, the police brought her to our local general hospital where she was treated overnight for severe dehydration. When she was brought onto our unit, she was strapped to a wheelchair and looked absent. She had on the typical hospital gown that covers the front of one's body and so little of one's back. I could see from the side that she had adult diapers on.

Margaret was a small woman in her early 40s with her hair closely buzzed. She was very thin and on her body I could see multiple scratches and bruises. In my years of admitting patients into the hospital, I had seen a lot of abuse cases. They typically included women with the left side of their face black and blue, and with bruises all over their bodies. Margaret was different; she had so many little scratches and bruises that I could not quite rationalize it.

During the admission process, she did not respond to any of my questions. My 11 pages of paperwork became limited to what I could observe. I felt free to skip questions that often seemed inappropriate at a time of admission, questions like: "When did you have your last bowel movement?" or "Are you sexually active?" I still wonder who composed those forms and whether they had ever provided useful information in an acute psychiatric hospital.

So with my determined mind, I kept asking over and over: "Has anybody hurt you?" I rephrased that same question every way I could think of. She did not react to my touch, so I held her hand and lowered myself to her eye level to ask the same questions repeatedly. When she got tired of my insistence, she indicated "no" with a gentle shake of her head. I was not sure that I had the truth, but I knew she could hear me.

I helped her get out of the wheelchair and walked her toward the bathroom. Her gait was steady and she needed no assistance to walk. Then I left her alone and waited outside, trusting that at some point she would get tired of waiting for me and would come out.

She did, all on her own. Outside the bathroom was a bed and she went and sat on the edge in a straight but not stiff manner and resumed her silence. I put the wheelchair away and did not put her adult diapers back on.

Per doctor's order, Margaret was put on a one-to-one, which is one staff member per patient for constant monitoring. Of course for Margaret it was a female staff member.

The next morning, when I came back on duty, the nurse reported that Margaret had gotten up by herself and gone to the bathroom on her own. She continued to refuse food and fluids, and she remained silent.

A week passed, during which Margaret had what is called a Riese Hearing, held inside the hospital. In a Reise Hearing the psychiatrist present a case to the judge to have his or her patient be medicated against his or her will. The hearing is held in what we call our Court Room, a big dark room with a large table in the middle and chairs all around. During that hearing the psychiatrist presented Margaret's case and the judge determined that she could be medicated against her will. From that day on when she refused oral medications with tight lips we had to do a "show of force," as we called it. We were to give her the fake choice of "you accept the injection or we hold you down for it." Each time she would resign in silence, lie on her bed on her side and expose her thin hip to us. It was sad to see her spirit being crushed and sadder to see Haldol, such an old-school antipsychotic medication, entering her body.

Intramuscular medications have a lot of side effects. The most common is akathisia, an inability to stay still. So the patients are observed pacing back and forth in the hallways. It is a feeling of loss of control that brings anxiety with it. The worst thing is that some of those side effects are irreversible, such as tardive dyskinesia, abbreviated TD, which causes involuntary movements, most often of the lower face. The constant repetition of involuntary protrusion of the tongue is the saddest thing to observe, especially when you know that it is induced by medications.

One other side effect, very quickly visible, is dehydration. In just a couple of days Margaret's lips became chapped and cracked. That probably helped her decide to start drinking and maybe eating a little. Her silence remained unbroken.

The doctor asked me to schedule a family session. In the chart I found a phone number and I called to organize it. The ex-husband, or ex-boyfriend, agreed to come that afternoon for the session. Our unit is locked on all sides so he had to wait at the door to be let in. He arrived on time with a young woman whose hair was buzzed like Margaret's. I let them into our Court Room, which we used at times for our family meetings, the same room where Margaret had her hearing the Monday before.

I invited Margaret to follow me into the room. With some hesitation we all found our places around the long table. Dr. L began by addressing the man, totally ignoring the young woman and Margaret. He explained the severity of her mental disorder and the evident need for long-term care. The man listened calmly and answered questions clearly.

He shared with us that Margaret had gone into the mountains many times to fast on a religious quest. "She usually comes back after two or three days" and added softly "but this time she didn't."

While the exchanges were taking place between the two men, I focused on Margaret's facial expressions. She seemed really attentive and present. Because of her visible grimacing at one point, it was clear to me that she did not agree with what her ex-boyfriend was saying. So, I interrupted the doctor politely and turned to Margaret, asking her if she would like to answer that question herself.

This was the beginning of her talking again.

Mildly surprised, the doctor turned towards her. Her head was down, avoiding all eye contact. At times she would rub her buzzed hair in an anxious way and continued staring at the table. He proceeded with his questioning, now looking at her. We didn't hear a full sentence coming out of her mouth but a whisper of "yes" or "no" at each question.

"Do you think it was dangerous to go for days alone in the hills above the town?" the doctor asked.

She shook her head and whispered a clear "no."

"Do you think it is safe to go for days alone in the hills?" he asked again.

She hesitated and said "no."

Dr. L had a small grin on his face, obviously satisfied that he had made his point. She clearly had no common sense and was mentally ill!

After the session, I walked her back along the long hallway leading to her room. I explained again my role as a nurse, stating that it wasn't part of my job to judge people.

I am on the unit to listen, offer some reassurance and try to understand. At one point she took my hand and thanked me in a full sentence and told me I had a beautiful soul. I smiled but knew it was the end of our conversation.

The next day, on a routine round, I entered the room and could not see her on her bed where she seemed to spend most of her days. It was not her habit to get out of her room and I was puzzled. Suddenly I saw two bare feet sticking out from the narrow space on the floor between the wall and the bed. My heart started to beat really fast. I approached with real apprehension. Margaret's little frail body, completely nude, was lying face down on the floor. She was startled when I asked if she was OK. There was no visible blood, no signs of distress, and I was relieved. I gave her a hand to help her get out of the narrow space. I wrapped one of her sheets over her shoulder and asked her if she could explain what she was doing. Again in full sentences she explained very clearly that she wanted to feel the cold floor on her body.

When she was done talking, I told her that I could see the appeal of that exploration, but reminded her that she was in a psychiatric hospital where her behavior was being watched. I reminded her that acting "normal" was her best choice to get out of here. With some difficulties, as if her face had not used those muscles for a while, she smiled.

Margaret stayed in the hospital for an additional legal hold of 14 days. She did not have any interaction with others except with her two daily visitors. During each conversation with me she became more talkative. She was still using very short sentences and still whispering. She talked about her spiritual research and her multiple trips to India. She seemed happy to know that I had also been to India. She talked about the year she spent in the Hindu hermitage of a guru named Sai Baba. She told me what she did, referring to walking in the mountains and fasting for four days as "pretty extreme."

One day, Margaret came to me to complain about the medication; she felt very anxious and could not think clearly. Her anxiety was visible. She was rubbing her buzzed hair back and forth with a very tense face while talking to me. I had no hope of the doctor changing her medication, so I asked him to add some Benadryl to help the side effects. This had a clear relaxing effect on her and she expressed gratitude to me for it.

After the 14-day hold ended, she signed an agreement to be a voluntary patient. She was no longer held against her will. She had regained the right to refuse medication but she stayed in the hospital and continued with her meds. On day 16, after she had a long visit with her young girl friend with buzzed hair, Margaret came to me with a special glow. She told me, in her soft voice, that she was ready to leave—and because she was a voluntary patient, she could.

Dr. L did not like to have to do a discharge that was not planned ahead. This one disturbed him. He requested from the discharging nurse the Against Medical Adivice papers and asked Margaret to sign them. When it was time to leave the unit, she came to me and pulled me towards her room to whisper a few last words. She said how grateful she was for my support. She asked me if I would be interested in reading a book about channeling that she and John, the ex-boyfriend, had written and published a while back. I told her that I like to read. She said that she would drop it off for me sometime.

She made it very clear to me before she left that she would not continue with her medication. I quickly explained to her about the importance of continuing Benadryl to reduce the very severe side effect that would happen while discontinuing Haldol abruptly. She asked pertinent questions and appeared to understand. She gave me a sweet hug with her still-frail small body as she left the unit. I thanked her for the deep sharing that she had done with me.

She left me with my head full of questions about what we call "religiously preoccupied" and "schizo affective." All those saints that I studied during my early upbringing in Catholic schools were extreme, too.

Eight months later, I ran into Margaret and her young friend in a large health food store in the same town. They looked happy to see me. At first I wasn't sure who they were. It took me a few seconds before the sight of their buzzed heads brought my memory back. They thanked me again and again: "You don't know the souls you touched," Margaret told me. She finally gave me the book she had promised.

I was left with a sweet taste in my mouth and a book about channeling, which I knew I would not read.

* * *

Kelly: Pushing out a drug addict

Early one morning, I was told that a young woman called Kelly was asleep on the floor in the first admission room. There are no beds in this wing of the hospital, where we first assess clients to see if they need to be hospitalized.

Kelly had been too delusional and incoherent to be assessed, so they just let her sleep. I made some coffee and around 9 o'clock I tried to wake her. A strong unpleasant body odor grabbed me at the throat when I entered the room. I am used to the smell of people who live on the street; a lot of patients arrive carrying that aura. Hers was a notch stronger and difficult to bear. She was lying on the floor with multiple blankets over her; her feet, as black as coal, were sticking out like two large logs. She did not wake-up at my first approach. On the second attempt, she moved a little and when I offered her coffee she requested tea with honey. A strange request but easy for me to adjust to. Back with the tea, I asked her if she could sit up so we could talk. She was a pretty blonde, slightly plump, dressed in army camouflage attire, a T-shirt and very old sweat pants that had been black in their younger days. She had multiple blisters and a cold sore on her bottom lip. I explained that my job was to assess her mental status and to understand how a young woman "end up" in a psych hospital.

With her sitting on the floor still rolled in hospital blankets, and me sitting a tolerable breathing distance away, I started my assessment. She answered a lot of questions with: "I don't know" in an irritated voice. I told her that "I don't know" was an OK answer, if she didn't know. She knew her birth date but could not tell me how old she was and mumbled "20-something" in a frustrated tone. She was delusional as she explained with great conviction that she could put her hand right through me.

As if to prove her statement, she reached her fingers towards my leg, I didn't move, controlling my impulse to withdraw and she gently touched my pants and stopped.

I asked her if she would try to go through doors or walls. She said "no" and mumbled something about evil, God, and peace in the world. It was difficult to follow her train of thought. Then she admitted using methamphetamine and got agitated saying the boyfriend who gave her the meth should be here instead of her. She hesitated and corrected herself: "my *ex*-boyfriend." I stopped my visual imagination from creating a matching boyfriend for Kelly.

Not really able to do my paperwork, I decided to let her sleep the meth off a bit longer. Around 11 o'clock, I offered food. She refused due to the blisters on her lips. She took tea again. I suggested a shower, and she nodded affirmatively. As we were walking toward the shower, I ventured to ask the most important questions of the assessment. I asked her if she wanted to kill herself or anyone else. She raised the sleeve of her shirt to show me a scar on her left wrist as an answer to the first question and denied wanting to kill anybody. She got into the shower room and started to undress. I went to our unit's "boutique," an elegant word to describe a small, dark room where the staff donates clothes for our patients, and got supplies for the shower. I don't like to give hospital pajamas to patients as it does not seem to help their self-image.

Back in the shower room, I put the "new" outfit on a dry shelf. She gave me her clothes that needed washing and her shoes so worn-out that there was not much left of them. She looked at them and asked me to toss them. She explained that her feet were too swollen to wear them anyway. I put shampoo on her hair and unwrapped the little soap bar to give her. She stayed under the water for a long time. It seemed to relax her. I let her be for a while. When I came back to check on her, I scanned her body and saw two large superficial cuts. One was about 40 centimeters long on her back, definitely not a place for a self-inflicted wound. Two more cuts on her legs seemed only a few days old and one more on her groin looked the most recent and most painful. I asked about the cuts, and she said that she did not know what happened.

I'd never seen anyone so young, so delusional, so destroyed, so pretty and so lost. After the shower, I offered her food again and sat with her to talk. She told me that it was still difficult for her to eat. Without much transition, she talked about her sexual abuse by her father, and in the same flow she gave me the phone number of her mother. She told me her real birth name, and explained that the name she had chosen to give us was that of her stepfather, a man whom she trusted.

I called the number that Kelly had given me, up in Washington State, and reached her mother directly. In my first sentence I said that I was with Kelly in a hospital and that she was safe. The mother's voice was shaken. Kelly had disappeared four years before and was on heroin last time her mother heard from her. She was so happy to know that her daughter was safe. The mother explained that she was in constant fear for her daughter's life, dreading the ring of her phone. She knew about Kelly selling her body for drugs. She volunteered that her daughter was welcome back home, but expressed doubt that Kelly would accept.

Now, freshly showered and with the new clothes on, she appeared less guarded; her hair did not look like a matted mess but like hair—shiny hair. I asked her if she was scared of being homeless and scared to see cuts on her legs that she could not explain. She said that she was afraid.

By noon two nurses came to escort her to the wing where she would have a room and a bed to rest. I had forgotten one paper so I followed them onto the unit. "Will I see you again?" she asked. I was surprised by the question, coming from someone who so recently had been a mix of delusion and anger. I said that I was not sure and told her she was in good hands. I put her old clothes in the washer and went back to the admission unit.

The next day, we had mandatory training in the hospital, so I was not working but I came by the unit to drop off a pair of shoes that my husband had agreed to give away. I knew they would be good for Kelly's blistered feet.

When I arrived on the unit I saw Kelly being escorted by a male nurse, walking in front of the nurse's station towards the laundry room. I followed them, feeling a little uncomfortable about being on the unit on a day I was not working and a little tense having to talk to a nurse I did not much confidence in.

I explained, in an apologetic way, that I had to toss Kelly's shoes, with her agreement, the day before, so I brought a pair from home. Kelly looked distressed. The nurse did not stop what he was doing—collecting Kelly's clothes and giving them back to her. Without taking the time to sit, just standing stiff, he started to read the discharge papers. He turned toward me and said, "She is to be discharged now."

I was stunned but didn't show my surprise. Kelly became defensive when the nurse explained—as if she was absent or just invisible—"She will not talk to the doctor, so she has to leave." Irritated, Kelly responded: "I just want to sleep," a logical answer for somebody crashing on meth. Looking towards me she said "You're the only one who cares around here." I was put in the very awkward position and quickly added, "We cannot help you if you don't see the doctor" and said "You have to get off your anger horse and learn to ask for help." The nurse, still standing holding the discharge papers, said, "She will go back to Washington to see her mother." I turned toward Kelly and added gently, "Your mom is really waiting for you."

There is a sense of success if we come up with discharge plans in the first 24 hours of a patient's admission. This one was just that—plus, shipping a really sick case across the state line is a fantastic way to save money. Just a bus ticket and the problem is solved! Our county hospital saves money and good luck, Washington, you are on your own.

I gave the shoes to the nurse. They had shoelaces and I could not give them directly to Kelly while she was on the unit. They both moved towards the doctor's office to sign the last papers.

I don't know what happened to Kelly. Did she even get on the bus? Our papers looked good, we had a safe discharge plan, but the reality is unknown. Maybe she is back on the streets, protected by her anger, her smell and her blisters, although I prefer to imagine that her mom took her in and kept her under her wing.

* * *

John: Living in your car is legal.

The one I "took home" in my heart this week was John.

John is a tall, handsome young man in his late 20s. His resemblance to Jesus Christ was probably due to his beard, his long hair and his thin-framed body. When I met him, John was still in his pajamas, but he looked clean and neat.

That morning I saw pictures in his chart, which is not really a common thing. Actually, it is not common for me to look at charts before doing my morning round. One picture, taken only two years before, was a family portrait of two parents and two brothers, each wearing a perfect smile. The two brothers looked so much alike that it was difficult to see which one was John: two clean-shaven, clean-cut American boys.

Another picture was of John's car, an old Oldsmobile with a piece of plastic covering a missing window. The car was no longer functional. The picture of the car's interior was one of real chaos; John had lived in it. The police report said that he was seen pushing the car to find a new place to camp. The report also stated that the individual living in the car had kept large cups of urine. Based on that observation they wrote a 5150, a legal hold for three days, for danger to self. Living in your car is not illegal but living in your car with large cups of urine will bring you to a psych hospital.

When the doctor and I saw him on the morning round, the usual questions were asked. John was very soft-spoken and answered everything appropriately. Very politely, he explained that it must have been a mistake.

"A lady told me I was going to get some help for one night and now, after five days, I am ready to go. Can I please have my shoes back?" John had something endearing about him, maybe it was his sincerity and gentle soul.

The doctor explained that she was recommending a second hold for him—14 days this time. In the end, John very politely explained again that he came for one night, and that he wanted to have his shoes back. After the interview, Dr. D exclaimed, "What a sick boy, very sick."

Later that day, I spent some time with John. I explained his legal status to him. He simply could not process this news, so I changed the subject and started to talk about the concern we were having about his choice of life that didn't "fit the norm." I asked about his car and questioned him about the cups of urine found in his car.

He explained that he was living the life of an Australian aborigine. The cups of urine were for his use at night and were to be "disposed of in the appropriate manner in the morning." The way he expressed himself and his vocabulary were surprising. He told me where he was finding food and where he was showering. With the same tone and matter-of-fact voice he said that he could hear the voices of the forefathers and the voices of the deceased.

During the conversation, he interrupted himself and looked away from me, apparently hearing something I could not hear. Then he reported to me what the voice was saying. His vocabulary was sophisticated but not always used appropriately. In one continuous flow, he was talking about the founding fathers and the book of the Egyptians. I have to admit that I loved listening to John. His mind was alive, rich and poetic. He loved the outdoors, the clouds, and couldn't imagine living inside a house.

I was so pleased that he was talking to me and tried to share some of his stories with Dr. D. She interrupted me almost rudely, saying, "Yes, I know, I need to increase his Haldol." In one sentence his gift to me had been crushed and bulldozed. There was no room for poetic ramblings.

Why waste time listening to someone who makes no real sense?

John did not fit in society. What happened after the perfect family portrait—a trauma? A bad drug trip? Who knows? I loved his conversations, his sharing and his gentle soul. That was his gift to me.

* * *

Tania: Lost custody

When I first met Tania, she was in a fetal position on her bed, her face turned away from the door. I introduced myself and she answered my questions with very short sentences or just a "yea" or "nay" if that would do. In the morning report I was told that we had to push her out of the unit, she was just too "comfortable."

A fetal position on a bed does not match my vision of comfort. If one's goal is to stay in a psychiatric hospital, there is something tragic right there and maybe we can try to find out why. So my approach was an attempt to understand. That morning I started with basic questions, just to connect: "How was your night?" and "how can I help you today?"

She started to open up a little bit. She was willing to agree on small goals for the day, like taking a shower. Taking a shower for this young woman of 25 years old was not a straightforward task. She had to request and get a new bag for her colostomy every day. Tania had survived a car accident when she was 18 and had to learn to live with that inconvenience. Her beautiful face had not been touched in the crash, but her gait was slightly uneven.

Before lunch was called, Tania told me that if she was discharged to a shelter, she would kill herself and she added that nobody would miss her. So I wrote that on her chart and told the doctor. She was not discharged that day.

On my second day with her, I brought some clothes from home. I didn't tell her that they were mine and also brought some hair conditioner with me.

"Why are you treating me so special?" she asked.

I told her that it was to show her that she was special and hopefully she would care for herself in that special way. She gave me a beautiful smile.

Little by little she unfolded her story. I was not eager to know, I was just present and she was gaining ease. She talked about her ex-husband, how he was able to afford a great lawyer and got custody of their four-year-old son. He had the job, the money, and that was enough to make him the right parent. She took a little picture out of her locker and showed it to me. The picture was a simple school photo all worn out at the corners. She explained how hard she had tried to get a job and a good apartment to get her son back. At every court date, she had lost the case. "So I went back to meth," she said in one dragging exhale.

I took the crumpled picture of her son and made an enlargement at the photocopy machine we have in the nursing station. To my surprise it came out pretty good, showing a cute little boy looking straight at the camera with a lovely smile. I asked her to write remarks all around the picture. Things like "I can do it" or "I will do it" or whatever she wanted to tell her son.

"I will love you and be there for you," she wrote around his cute little face. I asked her if she wanted to post this masterpiece inside her personal locker or over her bed. She picked over her bed. I taped it there and I went home.

On the third day I spent with her, I saw her opening up like a flower. She made phone calls. She found a sober-living bed without my help or the help of the social worker. She left the unit and gave me the biggest hug, saying "I will do it."

I felt warmth, and even though I didn't know about the next day I knew then that she had hope, trust and a warm heart inside.

* * *

Ben: A life sentence

The patient who upset me most and is still troubling me today is young, tall and skinny Ben, now in his second or maybe his third hospitalization. On his first visit he was elegantly handsome; now, after all the medication, he was starting to have a mask-like face, some stiffness of his arms while walking, and overall a medicated look.

The reason for his hospitalization this time, as before, was "overwhelmed with the voices." No God or Pope giving him orders, no paranoiac thoughts, just voices in his head.

During his first hospitalization he had shared little about his life. He had been living alone with his mother and he was spending hours staring at a young couple next door. From his window, he could see them coming in and out of their home and looking at them, he would imagine their conversations. After a while he did not need much imagination, he could "hear" them talk, he could hear everything they were saying and thinking. After that their voices would not leave his head, day or night.

He was hospitalized, diagnosed with schizophrenia, and medicated. Ben was smart enough to understand what it meant to be schizophrenic. He had worked as an aide in the mental health facility previously. He told me that he hated his diagnosis and that it wasn't a way to live.

I tried my best to give him some reassurance. Yes, being locked in a psychiatric hospital was maybe what we can call "hitting bottom" but maybe he would have the time here to imagine a different future. I was trying to give him back some power, recommending that he stay out of his room more often to hear real human voices.

Yes, it was difficult or even overwhelming, but he could think clearly and still have some power of decision.

To this day, I still wish that Ben would've had a different doctor. I know our medical director would initially have given him a diagnosis of depression with psychosis. Such a big difference of diagnosis: One is a temporary sad moment in one's life in which you are given anti-depressants for a few months that could give the voices a chance to disappear. The other diagnosis, schizophrenia, is a life sentence. It sticks to you wherever you go. You are put on heavy medications, which sometimes can help but they can also give one auditory hallucinations as a side effect. How sad!

During one of our conversations, Ben asked me to repeat a sentence I had just spoken. He admitted that the voices in his head were interfering with his listening to my voice. I empathized with him, guessing that it was probably difficult to have a couple talking in one's head. I could only imagine this and encouraged him to listen attentively to real people around him and accept the voices in his head as background noise.

I was in charge of the team that weekend, so I didn't have enough time with individual patients while also doing all the paperwork.

His mother came to see him each day. Their relationship seemed close; they played cards. Was she helping him? I didn't know, but her heart was with him, that I could feel.

When I came back the next week, the staff "from the other side" —the unlocked side of our hospital—came to our morning meeting. They are paper pushers: "utilization review," "nursing director," and so forth.

I read somewhere that in America there are eight paper pushers for each direct caregiver, so there are many of them. They care about charts and they don't even meet the patients.

Three of them came that morning and waited until we were all seated. Then the nursing director addressed the group. In a couple of short sentences, she explained what had taken place the previous night.

Ben had gone AWOL and committed suicide in the school nearby!

I was shocked. A janitor had found him hanging at the end of an electric cord. He had pushed his way passed one of the older nurses when she was going to a utility room in the back hallway. The overhead code gray was called. The staff thought he was contained in that hallway but Ben put all his energy into kicking in the last door. The magnetic lock let go and off he ran.

Once he was out, a male nurse in good physical condition chased after him for several blocks. There is a "no-hands-on" policy once a patient has gone AWOL, but the nurse was trying to save some time until the police could get there. The nurse was able to catch up and tried to reason with Ben, who had started slowing down to catch his breath. He heard the nurse's plea, but resumed his flight and disappeared. Later that day he entered a nearby school where he ended his life and his suffering by hanging himself.

Was giving him the diagnosis of schizophrenia a part of his death sentence? I don't know. I am just guessing that life without hope is not far from death.

* * *

Sage: Spiritual starvation

Sage was a man in his early 30s, looking extremely fit. At each break, instead of getting in line to be given one cigarette, he squeezed by all the patients and went to the sunny part of the patio to silently start what looked to me like tai chi. He had elegance, grace, concentration and strength. After the breaks, I saw him approaching each staff member, one at a time, trying to be heard. When it was my turn, he explained that he really wanted to tell me something important. I realized that giving him a passing ear would not work, so I scheduled the time to really sit down and listen to him all the way to the end.

After all the lunch trays were returned to the cart, we found a quiet corner in the community room and we sat down across from each other. I listened and observed. As he talked with intensity, his body moved with ease and suppleness. The front half of his head had been meticulously shaved up to a line going from ear to ear; the back was left alone, letting long brown hair grow down to his shoulders. I did not ask the significance of this peculiar hairstyle, nor did he offer an explanation.

It is not easy for me to recap this long monologue. I wish I could have taped it. He first gave me a little of his history. I did not have to ask questions, his thoughts were linear and chronology was the thread that he followed. He first shared that he was a successful special effects director and this was confirmed by his mother and sister. One day he felt empty inside and decided to go on a spiritual quest. He got into yoga, tai chi, meditation and tried a variety of other practices, including chanting.

At the end of a big job, he was offered a silo to take home—a hollow one that had been used in a movie. He managed to transport it and install it in his backyard. He built a suspended bottom so that he could sit inside and if he did not move he would find immobility and silence. He found that the silo was a perfect place to do his chanting, and quickly noticed that he could chant at the top of his lungs without neighbors complaining.

So he chanted for 16 years, inside the silo!

One day, he had a powerful insight and that is what he desperately was trying to share with anybody who would listen to him. He explained that something opened in him and he saw his connection to the universe. "You realize that the Bhagavad Gita, with its epic battle of Mahabharata, was really us and that each character was like a virus getting into oneself to create diseases. The battle was a test and if we were aware and able to really look at it, like grains of rice that are falling from above into our heads and body, then we could be connected to the Universe." As he was talking, he put both his hands on the top of his head with fingers all opened forming a cone shape and let his hands slowly drop to show the gentle caress of the rice falling from above covering him. "The observation and the awareness will prevent us from having disease inside our body." Barely catching his breath, he continued: "If the disease comes inside, again observation and awareness would be the only remedy against the invasion."

He had discovered the end of suffering and was ready to share it. He was visibly happy that he had found ears willing to listen to his powerful insight.

A couple of staff members passed by our table and gave me a look of "poor you, having to listen to this gibberish."

Because I took close to half an hour to listen attentively and I let him develop and share until the end of his story, he asked, with some trepidation, if I was getting it. I reassured him that I understood what he was saying.

When he heard me saying those words, tears rolled out of his eyes. I quickly added that maybe not everybody was ready to hear about awareness and observation.

I was trying to bring his mind back to our world, a concrete world with a door that opens if you say the right things or closes on you if you say the wrong things. I talked about his mother's and sister's concerns. Together, the two women had called the Crisis Team on his behalf, saying that Sage had stopped eating and stopped caring for his environment. When he told the evaluating staff that he did not need to eat food anymore, the assessment was suddenly clear that he could be locked up on a 5150, a legal hold for three days as a danger to himself. His hospitalization was only based on the basic need for food that he was denying himself.

He told me that he was ready to write a script about the virus and with his writing he could free men from suffering. I gave him some paper and a pencil and he immediately put his head down and started to write. When I left him, he looked relaxed and much calmer—as if he had an ally and that he had been heard.

I was quite delighted with his story. It was close to many of my recent readings. Somehow, somewhere he had crossed the line from reality to spirituality or sanity to insanity. When I left him, I impressed on him the importance of reassuring his family that he would resume eating. He did not resist and nodded that this was a detail we could agree on.

When I finished my third 12-hour shift in the hospital at the end of my week, I did my routine tour of the community room to say my goodbyes. The TV was on, filling the room with the usual outside tragedies. Sage was very calm, still sitting at our table with pages in front of him. He was very grateful when I approached him and offered me a shriveled business card with his name on it. I told him I really appreciated the gesture but I could not take it. He understood without any need for explanation. He mentioned that almost every day he was at a health center in a nearby town where he was teaching tai chi. I thanked him and felt a sense of sadness about not knowing what was going to happen to him. Sometimes I just miss the joy of opening our heavy doors to see the wind of freedom blowing onto those sensitive souls.

* * *

Melissa: Abused or delusional

Melissa was a 20-year-old from the Philippines, diagnosed with Schizo Affective Disorder, and was on Clozaril, the antipsychotic used as a last resort—a medication with pages of side effects, including hallucinations, increased heart rate and serious risk affecting white blood cell count which requires regular blood monitoring.

Melissa was so petite that from the back she could be mistaken for a 15-year-old girl. I cannot really recall when I first met her, because she had so many admissions with the same presentations. Each time she claimed that she had been raped—sometimes by the staff at her board and care, other times by the police who had brought her to the hospital.

The first time I had her on my load of patients, I took a whole day to approach her, just to establish a rapport of trust. She often seemed preoccupied and very busy. She was meticulous about her belongings, washing all her clothes daily. She slept with multiple layers of clothes and always with a light on. Those choices are red flags of abuse, something I had learned while working at an adolescent unit years ago.

In my first one-on-one conversation with her I invited her to come to the community room and had to wait for her to get ready. Every time she had to leave the room, the routine was the same: She had to make her bed army style, until one could bounce a coin on it, put her two slippers perpendicular to the foot of the bed and then she was ready.

Once we were sitting at a table in the community room, I asked my usual question about her understanding of why she was hospitalized. Without taking a moment to reflect, she explained that the reason she was here was because she had been raped in the presence of her brother. Then she went on, rambling about her father hitting her with a bar from the bed and then leaving her on the balcony for as long as three days. She mumbled "better me than my little sister," adding "That way I could protect her from my father."

I listened to her without any more questions and gave her all my attention and empathy for her suffering, real or not. I shared my suspicions of abuse with the medical doctor and the social worker, who both said that it was part of her delusions and that there was nothing to report. She was one of our regulars who six months before had been here with the same presentations.

The three days I had her on my load, I could see her pacing the hallway, giggling and talking to no one. I never saw her interacting with peers. Every day she would wash all her clothes and change her sheets. I continued to approach her gently, not demanding anything, just offering my help to keep her room tidy as she liked it.

On my second day with her, I sat on the floor of her room to connect with her. Again she started to talk about her father raping her and about the balcony episode. I was not sure how many times I could hear that story, so I suggested that she write it down and gave her paper and a pencil. I also suggested that she write about short-term goals and long-term goals for her life. She seemed pleased with the idea and she wrote three pages with our little hospital pencil and asked me at the end of our shift if I would like to listen to what she had written. I felt bad about having to say no, but I had run out of time to sit longer with her. I thanked her for wanting to share and said I would try to make time for her the next day.

My last day with her that week, IOn Sunday, I made time for her to share her writing and again sat on the floor to listen to a mixture of the balcony story, the rape, the abuse by her father, mixed with a car exploding, babies being killed, and about two pages of goals. She wanted to dance funk and return to school. She read all her writing of three pages without stopping. I thanked her sincerely for sharing her goals with me. She seemed really pleased and gave me one of her beautiful smiles.

Later that day, Melissa's mother and sister came to visit her. As soon as her mother entered the visitation area, I heard Melissa ask her if her father had hit her again. I discreetly looked at her mother and saw that she had a black eye perhaps a few days old. I did not hear her mother's answer. They sat at one of the tables and I left them some privacy, but maintained visual supervision at a distance. The visit lasted about five minutes before the mother and daughter asked to be escorted out. When I returned I found Melissa pacing the hallway and approached her cautiously to ask if she cared to share with me what had happened. She mumbled something about her mother denying all that had happened. This time she explained that her mother had tried to kill her with a knife and it was only because of the neighbors intervening that she was saved. Melissa seemed anxious and seriously preoccupied. I listened to her for a while and checked her pulse rate, which had risen to 138, so I notified the doctor. There wasn't much that he could do, because it was a side effect of the Clozaril she was on.

By the end of my shift, I could see Melissa watching television while still mumbling to herself. I tried to talk to her in simple words to offer reassurance: "You know you're safe here, nobody can hurt you."

She smiled, saying, "Yes, I feel safe here."

One side effect of Clozaril I know for sure is that the use of it makes me very angry. How can one assess someone under the influence of a drug with side effects of delusion and hallucinations? I really believe that Melissa had been abused, but now she was in a system where she had been labeled and there was nothing that I could do about it.

The following week I had Melissa again on my team. On my morning round, I found her all dressed, lying on her bed as usual. I told her that I would be her nurse for the day. She smiled, saying "You are the one that called me Princess."

It came back to me because I rarely use nicknames or terms like "sweetie" even with my closest ones at home, but the previous week while waiting for her to tidy her room and put her slippers perpendicular to her bed, I was holding the door and when she was finally ready, I had said "After you, Princess," saluting her on her way out. She had given me one of her radiant smiles and she had not forgotten that quick exchange.

All the nurses on the unit loved Melissa. She was such a cute one and "so sick," they all said.

I am left with my anger about the use of Clozaril and a deep sadness for Melissa.

* * *

Josh: Looking at anger

One morning when I got out of the nursing station, I
saw a young man reading the list of patients and staff that
we posted each day at the door. Only the first name and
the first letter of the last name are used on the list. The
patients are divided into four teams. Each team is made of
a psychiatrist, registered nurse, social worker and
psychiatric technician, called a "psych tech." The young
man turned his head towards me and asked "Who is on
my staff?" I asked him if his name was Josh and he nodded
affirmatively. I introduced myself, saying that I was the
nurse on his team for three days.

Josh was 19 years old, tall and quite a handsome
young man. His right arm was in a cast from hand to above
the elbow. I had been told that he would be my "project"
for the day. For some reason I got to be known on the unit
for being able to connect with angry young men. I am not
sure when all that started but it was now a given. Also, the
patients that spoke only Spanish were assigned to me for a
more obvious reason.

I had been told that Josh had been in five-point
leather restraints the day before and the day before that.
"Threatening behavior" was the term used on the chart.
On the unit, you can insult staff if you want to, but if you
use threatening words or make threatening gestures,
somebody will call a Code Grey and the staff will "control"
you. If you resist the invitation to calm down in your room,
you will be sent to the seclusion room. If you rebel there,
you will end up in leather restraints and get medicated.
Those are the choices, on the slippery slope of anger.

Looking at his designer sweatpants, I guessed that
Josh was from a well-off family. I also noticed that he had
difficulties standing still and I offered to walk the hallways
so we could talk. He started with a long list of complaints

about the staff on the unit. I listened and validated his feelings of frustration. I did not have to agree or justify the staff, I just listened as is always my first line of approach. The blaming game is often about the past so I try to bring patients back to the present with "How can I help you today?"

He wanted to be released from the hospital. That's all he wanted: to be released. We walked and talked, which sure gave me my walking for that day. Without too many questions on my part, he shared bits and pieces of his life. His first drug use was at age 14, after which he said he never stopped. He told me that he took all his mother's jewelry and sold it to a pawn shop for $500. He told the buyer that they were fake diamonds when in fact they were real. In return he got six balls of cocaine, eight of methamphetamine and some pot. He seemed to look for my reaction, perhaps to see a judgment from me, and when none came he continued to talk. He told me about being molested by his uncle when he was seven years old while his parents were on a cruise.

With time he arrived at the incident that brought him to my unit. He had wanted to visit his father. His father got a look at him and slammed the front door in his face. "So I smashed the window with my fist." He raised his right arm in its cast to show me the evidence of the blow. Damaged ligaments, cut nerves and maybe permanent loss of sensation in two fingers, this was the price of his anger that day.

I spent a lot of time with Josh. Listening, walking, validating his feelings and helping him to see which actions would serve his life. He cried like a kid, like the kid he was.

He came to my anger management group. When I asked him if an action based on an impulse of anger was serving his life, he said, "It felt better," then paused and added "for a minute." So I asked again: "Does an action coming from anger serve our lives?" He shook his head, and looked away for a second before saying, "No."

The next day, he asked me if we could have another anger management group. I organized my schedule to find time to do so. He came and was really showing interest. We looked at our common reactions when we are triggered. How fast we go into judgment and blame. They all knew that part. We looked at how we can get lost in revenge and forget about ourselves.

I noticed that he still had a difficult time remaining seated. He would sit for a while, then move, then sit down again. I checked his pulse; it was 100. His blood pressure was 168/100. I notified the psychiatrist, Dr. J, who told me that the high blood pressure was a medical problem, so he sent me to Margaret, the physician's assistant who does the history and physical examinations. Margaret told me that the high blood pressure was probably a side effect of the antidepressant. I was concerned for Josh. I did not like the ping-pong between doctors. I did not want to add my opinion, probably a misdiagnosed alcohol detox. So when they finally agreed on a small dose of Atenolol, I thought that it was better than nothing.

After working with him for two days—I mean listening, accepting who he was and helping him to shine the light on what was going to help him—he shared that he always wanted to be a pediatrician or maybe a psychiatrist. So I asked him what he wanted to do that day to take a step towards this long-term goal. He had some difficulty thinking of what he could do. It was so much easier to focus what the others were *not* doing.

He searched in silence and finally said that he wanted to regain total mobility of his arm. I really enjoyed seeing how real and vulnerable he was. He could easily have jumped into the old habit of placing blame, but he seemed to have gained awareness that it wouldn't help him. During our occupational therapy session he became irritable and on the signout sheet, he scribbled the "F" word and left the group. He came and told me what he had done. I asked him "Did that action serve your life?" Without a pause he said "for a minute!" and smiled.

Sunday was the end of my week of work. I had done my three 12-hour shifts. I told him I was not going to be back the next day; I was going to be off for four days. I acknowledged that I was too busy enjoying life to work more than three days a week. He invited me to say more about that. I told him about hiking, canoeing with my husband, playing the piano, riding my bike and more. He listened to me with gentle attention. At the end he leaned his head to the side and asked if he could get a hug from me. Confident that I was not crossing the so-called "professional therapeutic boundary," we hugged and I told him that I trusted him not to waste time on drugs but to make the right choice to find joy in his life. He smiled.

* * *

Eric: Finding a buoy for life

The police brought Eric in handcuffs and asked him to sit in one of the assessment rooms. He complied. He seemed jovial, had a clean haircut and was casually dressed but neat.

The police told us that he was a high suicide risk. He got himself demoted at work, from manager to sales assistant. He gave away most of his belongings and was casually planning his death with arsenic in three weeks' time. He wanted to finish paying his bills, get his Christmas presents for his family and then do himself in.

I sat down with him and the first thing he told me was that he would not talk to me. He was done talking, done with therapy, and nothing was going to make him change his mind.

I did my usual first interaction, offering food and drink. He asked for tea with milk. I left the room to make it. When I came back I started a small conversation about tea. After only a few words he said, "I will talk to you because you're funny."

I was not sure if his "funny" was meant as a compliment, or if it was I who was funny looking. I didn't ask and started my interview.

The questions were not only to fill up my 11 pages of assessment. I was really inquiring how a 41-year-old man ends up being brought by the police to a psych hospital?

He started to talk. For someone who didn't want to talk, I got more out of him than I ever asked for. He talked about his lack of trust since his last boyfriend cheated on him. His relationship with his mother was close and he talked with ease about his homosexuality.

It was not an easy issue even though he had been out of the closet since the young age of 19. I could not see any underlying depression or a real reason for him to be so done with life.

"I'm done with this life, no reason to be happy on this earth, I'm done. Done, and nothing will stop me," He said determinedly.

I listened and listened closely. I could not find anything to anchor his life down. No kid that he would want to see growing up.

At that point he talked about religion, he talked about the raptures. I shared my concerns regarding suicide and religion.

"I'm taking my chances. I might end up in hell but I might end up in heaven and there I will be able to do my real job: I will help others."

Finally, I had something. "Helping others" was something I could help him connect with. Something even I could relate to and try to bring him back to earth now and tomorrow. We talked for a while longer. He seemed to be reconnected with the feeling that comes with helping others.

Eric had health insurance and there was a bed at our local private clinic on the hill. He could be transferred. I filled in the transfer papers and stayed with him until transportation arrived.

We had connected deeply, even though we had not spent much time together. When he left he told me that he had done his talking with me and would not talk again to anybody else. I told him that we, people who enjoy helping others, thrive around people. At the clinic on the hill he would meet people with whom he could share his story and that it could maybe help them.

When he was on the gurney, ready to go, I told him I trusted that his life was not over because inside him was the powerful pull to help others and that it was what he was on this earth for. He looked me in the eye, stayed silent and gave a direct and sincere smile.

I am not sure if that little string of life was strong enough to hold him back. Was it the life buoy he could not find? It was a string of connections, a sweet and deep connection that had a life of its own.

* * *

Delilah: Voices from heaven

On Delilah's legal hold, I read that she stayed in her car for three hours and "became angry when approached." Because she had no visible plans to care for herself, she was transferred to our psychiatric unit for a three-day evaluation.

Delilah was a petite Filipina in her late 30s. She was wearing her thick black hair down to her shoulders. On my morning round—right after 7 a.m., when I check on all the patients—I found her on her bed with all her clothes on. It was too early to engage in deep conversation, but her answers seemed appropriate. They were very short and when the conversation appeared to reach an end she walked out of her room, giving the clear message that she was done. During the day I saw her pacing back and forth in the hallways, difficult to say if she was just stretching her legs or trying to deal with an interior agitation. I did not observe her having any interaction with other patients and she appeared to be resisting my approaches.

Later that day I thought about asking a coworker, also from the Philippines, if she could talk to her in Tagalog. She came back soon saying that Delilah's answers were appropriate, brief and that she walked away as soon as the conversation seemed to arrive at an end.

Since the day of admission, Delilah had not showered. She was wearing the same yellow dress she had arrived in. When I offered clothes from what we called "the boutique," she politely refused and walked away.

The second day when I was with her, I offered her the opportunity to use our free phone if she had anyone she would like to talk to. She accepted without hesitating.

Patients always have access to pay phones in community rooms, but they rarely have the coins for the calls. In the admission room there is a free phone which patients can use at the discretion of a staff member. Delilah followed me through a pair of locked doors into the admitting room as I picked up a consent form.

To give her some privacy, I stood at the door. Her conversation seemed friendly and her voice calm and reassuring. When I sensed that the conversation was coming to a close, I asked Delilah if I could talk to her friend. She agreed and signed the legal consent form so I could talk to Alberto.

He turned out to be a good source of information. He was an older man, probably in his 80s, and seemed deeply caring. He had met Delilah eight years earlier when she was working as a home caregiver for an elderly lady across the street. He knew that Delilah had been doing home care for many years and also that she had a history of schizophrenia, but in all those years she had always kept her job. The last home care job ended the previous week when the old man passed away. She was still getting her mail at Alberto's, so she came once a week to collect it and visit with him.

The ice was broken. Now I had a subject to discuss with her. We talked about Alberto and how important it was to have a friend. She seemed happy to talk about him. We also talked about her last job and how hard it was to let go of a person one cares for. When I felt that the trust and ease were there, I asked her again what her understanding of this hospitalization was. She explained "I forgot my wallet at home and I ran out of gas so I stayed in my car."

I asked her what was the story about the glass of water she had thrown at someone who had offered her a drink when she was in her car. She explained that it had poison in it. I nodded and reassured her that in the hospital the water was safe to drink.

Later that day, Alberto called me. I asked him to convince Delilah to shower and that it was important to show that she could take care of herself. He was surprised, saying that she was usually a clean person.

After the phone call she asked to take a shower. I smiled, thinking of Alberto, and provided her all the supplies before unlocking the door for her. A few minutes later the shower emergency alarm resonated in the nurse station. We went to the indicated hall way and found Delilah standing in a dry shower, in the dark, pointing at the smoke detectors, asking if they were cameras. I reset the alarm that she had pulled. I explained that what looked to her like cameras were smoke detectors and she seemed to believe me.

After the shower, in clean clothes, she sat with me in her room. I asked her if she understood the term "gravely disabled," which was written on her legal hold. It wasn't clear to her so I gave her the definition and asked if she could provide the "basic needs of food, clothing and shelter for herself." She answered, "I am not rich, but I have plenty of money in my account, and Alberto told me I could stay with him until I found another home care job."

Then she added, "There are a lot of home care jobs and I have good references."

The next day I took her to have her daily evaluation by the doctor. She sat on the edge of her chair and immediately began explaining that she had a place to stay, and had lots of money in her account. The doctor joked, "If you have so much money, I should marry you." I was shocked by this inappropriate joke and to my surprise she answered, "If you marry me for my money, I will marry you for your body." They both laughed and I was glad that she had a sense of humor—it was definitely far from mine. I changed the subject to the discharge plan.

After the session with the doctor, I stayed a little while with Delilah. She was talkative and pleasant. She talked about her schizophrenia: "I hear voices from heaven." She leaned over the big table that was separating us to get closer to me and asked in a soft voice, "Do you have schizophrenia too?" with her finger pointing at the ceiling.

I told her that I didn't but that I was trying very hard to understand what it meant. I hadn't finished my sentence when she answered, "I know. I can feel it." I'm not sure what that meant, but it was something that felt like a connection.

From that point on Delilah was friendly and talkative with me. She said that because of her schizophrenia she couldn't get married, but that was OK with her. She also became physically comfortable with me, giving me hugs at the end of each shift. She was put on a low dosage of antipsychotic; I don't remember if she was legally obliged to and had signed a consent form.

Delilah was discharged during my off time. One nurse told me that she had looked for me to say goodbye and to tell me how much I had helped her. I'm not sure what she meant. I guess I showed real interest in her. I didn't judge her and didn't fear her.

The weekend following her discharge she called the unit asking to talk to me. Her voice was very excited, saying that she was doing well and had a job. She called to thank me for my help and said that she was taking her medications and that she had a new cell phone which she was testing on this call. Her laugh was loud and sincere. She caught me by surprise and I hadn't had time to show much emotion, but I told her that I was very touched by her call, as I sincerely was.   * * *

FTW: Vision of anger

After a sabbatical year in Europe, it was strange to be back in this locked facility—strange and yet so familiar.

Our unit is a short-term facility, meaning that most people are on a three-day legal hold, called a 5150. A psychiatrist can request to extend the stay with an additional hold; a 5250. A court, with the patient present, will uphold or deny the request. The average stay of our patients is under two weeks.

So I was a little surprised, after a year of absence, to hear my name called by a patient when I got on the floor. We did the small talk, the exchange of smiles, and I continued my morning round. He was what we call a "regular."

The first one I brought home "under my skin" that first day back at work was not assigned to me, so I knew very little about him. When I first saw this young man in the hallway, he was arguing very loudly with the doctor and already had a couple of male staff members by his side. He was standing up, arching his nude torso; his thin hips were barely holding up his jeans, staying on maybe by habit. His tone was building up rapidly. I could predict what was going to happen and decided to do "crowd control." A group of patients were gathering around as the voices were growing louder. I directed the patients back out of the hallway into the community room.

When I returned the young man was in five-point leather restraints, attached to the bed in the seclusion room, asleep. He got what we called a "cocktail" or a "five-one-one," (5 mg of Haldol, 1 mg of Cogentin and 1 mg of Ativan), which is only given when justified by threatening behavior.

I walked into the room with my colleague who had him assigned to her load of patients. The door is left open when a patient is in restraints and a staff member sits at the door watching at all times. In the room there is only one heavy wooden bed, securely attached to the floor. For the first hour, a nurse comes every 15 minutes to assess the patient's circulation. This is done by sliding two fingers between the leather and the skin at the wrists, the ankles, and by observing the color and temperature of the limbs. The restraint on the chest must be loose enough to allow a hand to slide under it. The check is done swiftly as a gesture done often and mechanically.

After the procedure, I glanced at the face of our young man. He looked so young, so calm and child-like. With the anger and the tension gone from his face, the lines on his forehead had disappeared. He was still without a shirt and my eye caught a glimpse of something red on his stomach, I knew it was blood, dry blood. I saw the letters "FTW" freshly carved into his pale young skin with the T being slightly taller than the other two letters. The carving had probably been done with a paper clip found somewhere on the unit. I heard my own voice reading softly out loud the three letters while trying to guess their meaning. My colleague hearing me helped me by whispering "Fuck The World." I was stunned, as if my mind could not absorb the message. I remained silent with a heavy weight on my own chest. I then noticed two thin fresh scratches on one side of his neck and saw that he had a swastika on his right arm. That was anger written all over him—pure, powerful anger, so much of it that his own blood was dripping out of him.

I was not there when he got released from the seclusion room. He was probably asked the routine questions about his understanding of the incident that brought him to restraints and was probably asked to verbally contract to do no harm. After a "cocktail " it is easy to agree with eyes half closed and nodding, just to be able to go back to a bed without restraints to crash again.

He did not show up at my anger management group that day, so I had no opportunity to get to know him better. He was just a vision of anger against the softness of his youth; a vision of a young man with no name, who melted my heart.

* * *

Buzzed: Longing for love

The one who is sticking in my brain and my heart tonight, I don't remember his name. He was a very tall young man, his hair was buzzed and he had a couple of bandages on the left side of his forehead. He came to my anger management group that morning.

I really like to start my groups with concrete examples from daily life. A lot of the patients have roommates, so one of my favorite examples is the dirty kitchen. I start with a clear description to help them visualize: "You wake up and find spaghetti all over the stove and a pile of dishes in the sink." I get very active participation from the group when they can relate to a common, frustrating situation, especially if there is somebody to blame!

So I write down on the board the judgments that our brain can find so easily to blame. We imagine the roommate getting up and the conversation starting. We look at what happens when we express blame, insults, etc. Do we really get what we need? Is the clean kitchen the only thing we want?

Then, I ask what need there is underneath that frustration. The participation slows down. I get the "what are you talking about" look on some faces. A few, ready to explore more, guess at "a need for participation, help and support."

Based on those needs, so often common to all of us, I ask them to imagine a conversation with a roommate. Sometimes they hesitate or they suggest "How about some help with the kitchen, man!"

I ask what gives them a better chance to be heard "you are a lazy slob" that was written on the board at first, or "I need your help." The response is usually unanimous!

That day, I had great participation from the group, so I asked if somebody would volunteer an example of anger of frustration we could look at. A tall skinny young man raised his hand and after I nodded to go ahead, he started to explain that after 13 years in jail he met a woman who became "his woman." They spent months together and he left for a few days on a job to find upon his return that "his woman" had had an affair with his best friend and cousin. He paused and said: "I took care of them both and then I went home and swallowed all the meds I could find. They pumped my stomach and I ended up here."

I was surprised by the intensity of his example. I was used to hearing something more along the lines of "the morning cigarette break is posted as 10 a.m. and the staff didn't open the door on time, and that pissed me off."

So I asked the tall skinny man to come and sit by me to explore with him his thoughts and judgments when he came home. Little by little we went from anger toward the others to a deep disappointment inside. He paused and expressed his sadness about the loss of his woman. Once he was in touch with his sadness he seemed calmer. He sat there repeating the word "sadness," as if it was a new feeling.

Then I asked what happens when we are sad. When he was grieving a loss, what he was longing for? He reflected and said easily, "We need support, we need to share what we went through" and added "maybe we need to be loved again."

I was surprised how fast that tall skinny gang member was able to see steps to get out of anger, to connect with sadness beneath it and to see what he was longing for. His body was more relaxed, he was more himself—his sensitive, real self.

The group was over, the patients left and he stayed a little bit longer with me. I tried to offer some more listening but he did not need to talk more. He just sat there, just absorbing the visible, comfortable reconnection he felt, the sweet power of knowing what he was longing for.

* * *

Tim: Not an absentee father

Most of my patients arrived at the unit yelling all sorts of things. Often they were handcuffed and sometimes even shackled. That is the way Tim arrived at my unit.

He was a tall, skinny 26-year-old man, very disheveled, who had destroyed property at his girlfriend's home. He had also thrown the TV set through the window of their second-floor apartment. That poor decision gave the cops grounds to write a legal commitment to a psychiatric unit on a 5150, a three-day legal hold for danger to others. The report I got said that it took a couple of police officers to contain his rage. He remained uncooperative with the police during his transfer and during their arrival at the hospital, so he became what we call a "direct admission," which is escorted directly into our unit, skipping the assessment unit that would give him a slim chance to have his legal hold broken by a medical doctor.

Being held firmly on one side by a cop and on the other by a health technician, he was clearly encouraged to sit on the bed of a seclusion room. I asked Tim if I was safe in the room with him. He gave me a very surprised look and replied "of course." With a little head nod, I gave my OK for the policeman to remove the handcuffs. While being compliant with the release of his wrists, he continued to voice anger towards his ex-girlfriend, repeating "You don't understand" and "You have no right to lock me up."

I felt safe enough to be with him alone as he was sitting and his voice was not as loud as before. So I allowed the staff to leave. They all went back to their assignments on the unit. Only the health technician assigned to my team stayed at the open door of the seclusion room.

I listened, most interested in gaining some understanding, without wasting time on judgement. I knew I had only one side of the story, so how could I judge or pretend that I knew something about his life. He began telling me his version of the story. How his ex-girlfriend reported to the social services that he was using meth. That report meant that he would probably lose custody of their four-year-old son. He expressed a lot of anger at her, slipping into the blame game like into an old pair of slippers. At one point he protested: "I don't want to be an absentee father, like my father was."

I guessed that this was possibly the root of his anger—the fear of being an absent father, like his father had been. I just had to help him see how important it was for him to be a father. As I was talking about this deep value of his, I saw his whole body transform, like a plant getting water. He stood up straighter and talked about his son, his joy, and what kind of father he wanted to be. Then as if grounded in deep value, he came up with all the strategies to move forward. For me this was the clarity of action that comes with a deep connection, connection with what is important to us.

He was going to call the social services, he was going to give urine in a cup every week, he was going to be a father. It was like I didn't exist anymore, he didn't have to fight me anymore, or fight anybody else, he saw what was really important to him and there was no turning back.

Tim never came to my anger management group. He stayed the three days required by his legal hold, spending time on the phone planning his next step. He was calm and determined and left the unit walking straight up.

I never saw him again.

* * *

Kyle: Histidine or first break

Kyle had never been in my anger management groups before.

On his first day in the community room, there were almost a dozen patients, a few visibly eager to start the group and a few others just sitting quietly, too medicated to have anything to share. Anger, one of my favorite subjects to explore, seemed to be quite relevant for a lot of the patients. Too often it is a big part of their lives. Their living conditions—with roommates that they can barely tolerate, the lack of jobs and low self-esteem that goes with that—all are good triggers for frustration and anger. Of course being locked in a psychiatric hospital with all kinds of restrictions is another perfect trigger to awaken the tiger in them.

Together, starting with very concrete examples from everyday life, we look at frustration and anger. We see how fast we are at judging and blaming, often skipping the listening that would lead to understanding, the deep listening to the pain in us and guessing other's pain. We look at the words that we use to block communication, like "always" or "never." I asked the question: "Did the action taken while you were angry really make your life better?"

That day, during the hour with the group, Kyle sat quietly in the back. He seemed to follow my words and my writing on the board attentively. At the end, as the patients were leaving the room, he approached me and said something I was unable to hear completely, so I asked him to repeat what he had said. Still in a very soft voice, he asked if I could meet with him in a quiet place, privately. I didn't know anything about him, only what I could observe in front of me: a young man well dressed and, looking his best with a recent clean haircut, well taken care of. The best I could offer, to feel safe and to give him the privacy he was asking for, I opted to talk to him in a quiet hallway. Together we walked past the nurse station and the community room and I leaned against the wall to show him I had arrived at our "private place."

Not wasting any time he started talking: "Do you think there are people who cannot express themselves?"

I was a little surprised by his question. Was that his question that needed so much privacy? Was he talking about himself? Was he looking for acceptance for who he was? Was he saying he was different?

He added, "For some, writing makes it easier."

I readily agreed. I didn't have a lot of time to explore his deep questioning and gave him a vague—and, to him probably, a weak—answer, mostly because I had other patients to take care of. I gave him a few sheets of paper and a pencil, which he accepted with a gentle smile, and I returned to my work.

Later in the day, as I was passing two large doors using the clicker attached to my identity badge, he quickly slid himself in behind me. Just a second of inattention on my part and he was in a hallway where he did not belong. Our unit has two sets of doors everywhere, so now he was still locked up, but in a seclusion room hallway. He did not confront me in any way, when I asked him to turn back to the unit where his room was and he obeyed my order without resistance. This incident, I am embarrassed to admit, happened a second time with the same elements of inattention on my part and swiftness on his, but again with no resistance to my request to return. I went to his chart and put a sticker to flag him as an "AWOL risk."

The next week, I was surprised to see him still on the unit. He did not fit the profile of a patient that needed more than a three-day hold to reset his mind to fit back into the outside world.

He was still the same quiet, young, surfer-looking guy that I had met the week before. Now he was on my team but still not my assigned patient. I heard Dr. V using the famous and sad term "first break." Because he was so delusional when he came in and because no drugs were found in his urine, there was only one way to explain why he thought the whole world was after him.

The famous "first break" drags with it the heavy diagnosis of schizophrenia.

Yes, he was of an appropriate age and the delusions with a zest of paranoia clearly pointed to one word: schizophrenia. When I looked at his chart, I wondered why somebody so young, apparently well and functioning, could just leave the world of common sense.

I sat down and tried to talk to him. It didn't have the effect or lack of effect that other mentally ill people would show. He was reserved, quiet, with good eye contact and all his responses were appropriate, at least during the time we had together. I had a few words with his family. His father mentioned that Kyle had finished college-level calculus and geometry and was wondering if stress could cause someone to just lose his mind. Kyle had two families and both sides appeared to be sophisticated people. They took turns visiting him. One of the days the mother and the father were there together, and they seemed cordial toward each other.

The mother called me one day, after visiting hours, to ask me to make an addendum to his chart. She had checked both sides of the family and there was no mental illness, contrary to what had been said before. The aunt mentioned in the chart had been hospitalized for depression and not schizophrenia.

So I continued to talk to Kyle. My curiosity was not threatening to him so he easily shared his feelings. He told me a lot about his life, his relationships or lack thereof. He also told me that for months he had been taking a supplement to gain muscle mass. He readily admitted that he was taking much more than the recommended dose. Continuing to show a gentle interest in his story, I asked the name of the product and wrote it down on a corner of my clipboard.

After our conversation, I went to see the doctor and told her about his overdosing on the supplement. She knew about it, saying: "It is only a supplement, you cannot overdose on it."

I didn't feel heard, so I kept my inquiry alive. I talked to Kyle's mother and asked for a list of the ingredients of all his supplements. I talked to Steve, an RN who was into weightlifting, and he told me that overdosing could be a real concern.

Later that night, at home, I took the list of ingredients and looked them up. "Creatine overdose: intestinal distress or diarrhea," and then another and another, until I got to "Histidine for growth and repair of tissue" and there it was: "Too much Histidine may lead to stress, mental disorder such as anxiety or schizophrenia." Steve was right! The overdosing was definitely a concern. Wow, a product that, if you did not follow the dosage correctly, would give you muscle mass gain and mental disorder as a bonus—what a deal! I thought about Kyle and his advanced math classes, thinking his math did not help him much this time.

The next day, I talked to his mother and to him as well. I didn't come from a place of "I know" but from a place of "maybe." I did not want to contradict the doctor. I still could feel the ghost of schizophrenia hanging around us while we were talking. The mother was extremely receptive and attentive to my words. I did not want to give her false hope. I just wanted to share what I had read.

A couple of days later, Dr. V was off and Dr. J discharged Kyle, saying again with a deep concerned voice that it was his "first break" and we would surely see him again. At this point Kyle did not meet any more criteria for a hospitalization so his mother came and picked him up.

One week later, we got a big bouquet of flowers from the family with a thank you note and my name on it. I took it as a good sign and never saw him again.

* * *

Helene: Government center

At 44 years old, very tall Helene was dressed provocatively in very short shorts that revealed all of her long legs. She was well groomed with nails painted, hair down to her shoulders with her permanent slightly outgrown. On approach, she was pleasantly polite.

I asked her if she could tell me her understanding of why she was hospitalized. She explained that her husband thought since she had been hospitalized once before, he could call the Crisis Team whenever he had a problem with her and that she would then be readmitted.

"That's all" she added calmly as if she had the complete evidence of truth.

On her chart the diagnosis noted was "bipolar." I asked if she thought that she had trouble with mood swings.

She denied ever having mood swings, quickly adding that the only one with mood swings was her husband.

Having some time on my hands, I sat down at a table to talk to her in the community room to explain what bipolar disease was. She was attentive and asked good questions. She was very thankful, saying that it was the first time that someone had explained to her what bipolar meant, adding that she had never experienced episodes of mania.

The longer I stayed and listened to her, the more bits of information came to me. She told me in passing that she suspected that her mobile home park manager had killed three elderly people to take possession of their trailers. I continued to listen as more suspicious information came out. The biological father of her adopted daughter wanted to kill her. At this point I did not have to believe or not believe. I was just listening and accepting that what she was saying was her truth. I then asked her what she wanted me to do with this information. She replied that she had tried to tell people about it, but nobody wanted to do anything about it.

Later that afternoon I was told that a police officer was coming to the hospital to interview her. Without hesitation or resistance she signed a consent form. We passed locked doors and entered a small room without windows, where the officer came and joined us to start his interview. I was there to supervise the visit and sat next to Helene in silence.

The officer asked her what she was doing in the Government Center at 11 o'clock at night, looking through files. She apparently had hidden in a toilet until the Government Center had closed and was found looking through the files by a night security person to whom she said that she was from the District Attorney's office.

The police officer said: "Mrs. H, we know that you don't work for the DA's office, so can you explain what you were doing here after hours in the Government Center?" Without hesitation Helene answered: "I was looking for forms." And then pragmatically added: "It is a family matter."

In just a couple of sentences the conversation seemed to have arrived at an end. Helene was ready to repeat her answer once more, but the officer could see that that was all he was likely to get and he ended the deposition and left.

I escorted Helene back to her room. I was smiling inside, being reminded again that I can only keep my genuine curiosity about people, but never pretend to understand them.

* * *

Weston: Catatonia or drugs

My first visual image of Weston is that of a young, handsome man standing in the middle of a hallway with an adult diaper down to his feet, the blue hospital gown barely covering his privates. Not a great look for a 19-year-old man.

He was given the worst diagnosis you can get: schizophrenia, catatonic type. It was a rare diagnosis as in most cases patients are not completely mute and unresponsive. Since Weston had the label of "catatonic," meaning "unresponsive," nobody on the unit was talking to him.

When I first met him as a patient, his eyes looked towards the ground most of the time and he did not respond to any of my questions. To get him to shower, one had to physically take him by the hand, put him under the warm water, give him soap, a washcloth and tell him to wash himself. He did not resist directions, he just did not respond. Eating was a concern too, as he was very skinny and was only nibbling at the hospital food we were putting in front of him. He completely ignored the fattening shakes that were added to his diet per doctor's order.

I looked into the chart and found out that it was what we call his "first break." I also read that he was into sports—especially basketball, which is not my favorite subject through which to connect with someone. I questioned a nursing friend and with my bright new limited knowledge of basketball I asked Weston a couple of questions. I got a small facial expression that gave me the clear sign that communication was possible. Quickly reaching the end of my basketball conversation, I told him that I had just returned from a ski weekend and asked if he was a skier.

"No," he said. "Snowboarder."

Well, in my opinion this was a conversation. So I continued going on about my skiing weekend, talking about the quality of the snow. He began putting words together. His sentences were still very short but totally appropriate and I was thrilled to be able to converse with him.

From that point forward I engaged Weston whenever we met, even when he was not assigned to me. One day, he shared with me that he could hear voices. I explained about people having to fight different battles and his was to learn to live with his voices. I said that maybe the medications would help, but that he had to do his part too.

His sentences grew longer and the staff, seeing me talking to him and walking up and down the hall with him, started to casually engage him too. There was no reason for him to wear adult diapers. He admitted later that he had given up. I did away with the diapers and reminded him to use the toilet every three to four hours. Then I stopped reminding him and he stayed dry.

The heavy diagnosis he had received is given when the possibility of drug-induced psychosis is eliminated, as these drugs can put people in a state of catatonia.

I was curious about his drug history. The hospital always tests for drugs when somebody comes in in an unresponsive condition. The routine tests are for alcohol, amphetamines, benzodiazepines, marijuana, cocaine and opioids. None of these were found in his urine. The parents said that he never used drugs, a common answer coming from parents. The only explanation for his state of unresponsiveness was the first break of schizophrenia catatonic type.

One day, a couple of young men were visiting Weston. I made sure to escort them out of our locked unit and while we were walking along the hallway leading to the last door, I dared to ask them if they knew if Weston had taken drugs. They smiled and said that "he used everything." Since I lacked a release of information from Weston to talk to his friends, I could not put this information in my notes. I told the doctor about my finding, but she shrugged her shoulders and returned to her chart. I knew that my information was too slim to affect the heavy diagnosis burdening Weston.

The next weekend when I arrived on the unit and we made eye contact, he smiled. He was watching TV looking comfortable. His parents and his younger sister came to visit, but he didn't seem very communicative with them. He did not return his mother's hug and his arms remained limp by his side. I could sense his mother's pain. With me, he continued to answer all my questions in short answers with his eyes gazing back at the ground, his comfort zone.

I asked him to reflect on his life: how he got to the hospital and what he envisioned as a next step. He appeared open to reflection. He was still on heavy medications and it was hard for him to wake up in the morning, but by afternoon he came out of the fog.

During my last evening round, I walked into the community room and noticed him watching two patients playing ping-pong. I asked him, "Are you going to join the game?"

He gave me a small smile and just said, "Soon."

* * *

Jack: Failing heart

I had known Jack for several years. He was a 42-year-old, slightly chubby Puerto Rican man with multiple piercings on his ears and some on his eyebrows. His hair was down to his shoulders.

He had one of the worst childhood histories I had ever heard, maybe because I spent a day with him at the ER when his blood pressure was dangerously high and I had the time to listen to him.

When he told me about his childhood, tears came to his eyes. Years of abuse, both physical and sexual. He could still hear the sound of his own head hitting the walls when his father was disciplining him. So difficult to imagine without tightness to my chest.

His teacher at school suspected the mistreatment but Jack denied it for years. As a child he was never allowed to wear shorts, to make sure the belt marks would not show. Until one day, when his father almost killed him and, fearing he might die, dropped him off at the ER.

He never saw his father again. The father went to jail and Jack wound up in a foster home. He was so skinny, so undernourished, that he started to overeat and become bulimic in his foster family. Then he got seriously into drugs, mostly meth.

At age 42 Jack is what we call a "repeat," a "personality disorder," a "drug addict." At this admission he was complaining about hearing voices telling him to kill himself by hanging. He was a mess.

The years of meth had done severe damage on his heart. He had a triple bypass but still required nitro on almost a daily basis. Due to his diabetes he told me that no doctor wanted to repeat the surgery that he needed for his dying heart.

His medical condition was so complicated that even after being clean now for the past three years he became homeless and his eight-year-old daughter was put in a foster home. I don't know what happened to his two other daughters and to his son, but he felt helpless and hopeless.

We had a long talk about the past that nobody can change, but when I tried talking about the future he knew that it was so short in time that there was no room for real hope.

I did not try to give him a pretend hope. I just made him feel that I enjoyed his company, and I did. That was our gift.

* * *

Vanessa: Cheated at age 2

The young woman, Vanessa, came onto the unit looking as if a train had hit her. The left side of her face had severe bruises, her temple area was so swollen that her eye was almost shut. Both her arms were also bruised and had superficial scratches. A gauze bandage covered her left wrist. She was in our unit because she had cut her wrist and had required 16 stiches.

During the morning report I was told that Vanessa had been so loud on the unit that it became a problem. She was my patient so I was asked to "control" her before we would get into more problems.

That morning, before I had time to say my name, she approached me pointing out a woman walking peacefully away from us, saying, "If you don't keep her out of my room, I am going to kick her ass."

The little old woman was known on the unit for being a "wanderer." She had Korsakoff Syndrome, also known as wet brain, from years of alcohol abuse and spent most of her days looking for her bedroom.

In the chart I read that social services had been involved in Vanessa's life since she was two years old. Her mother, a prostitute, had left her in a hotel for two days with only a couple of sandwiches. As if the road behind her mother had only one straight line, Vanessa was later diagnosed with HIV and hepatitis C, a gift from her ex-husband or former boyfriend, now in jail.

Vanessa did not want to talk about her assault. She kept saying "my friends took care of it," as if her world was separated from ours, without the same justice, or the same laws.

It was not easy to reach her. I tried and I must say I almost gave up more than once. I knew the insults were coming from her suffering but it was hard to bear, it was exhausting. I had other patients to take care of and I could feel myself wanting to flee from her approach. Coming out of her mouth were insults, complaints or demands. I stayed grounded and did not let the insults get in. She insulted what I represented while knowing nothing about me. I was just the face of the system that took her freedom away, a system that had failed to protect her. I continued to treat her like any other patient and gave her clothes from what we pompously called "the boutique," a room full of donated clothes from the staff. I also administered painkillers when she was in pain, gave her extra pillows and told her I was available if she needed to talk.

For her daily dressing change on her wrist, I asked Vanessa to follow me to the treatment room. Together we walked along two hallways, going through large locked doors. She remained cooperative. I took my time, so as not to not hurt her. During one dressing change, I let her know how difficult it was for me to reach her. I asked again if she would be willing to talk to me. To my surprise, she accepted.

We walked back to her room to find a quiet place. She sat on her bed and I leaned against the wall across from her and let myself slide down to the floor to sit across from her. There were no chairs in those rooms, lest they be used as weapons. She started to talk and talk and I gave her my full attention. A lot of blame and frustration came out first. After some time she was able to reach behind her anger, to sadness, very deep sadness. She became a child that just needed to cry softly—so much sadness and so many reasons to be sad, an awful past and a gloomy future.

I asked her if she wanted to spend all her energy fighting others or if it was time to start caring for herself and to start accepting support. Her defenses were crumbling, her shell began to vanish. There was a palpable shift in the room. A new trust began to grow. Her real desire, her real goal—the one down in her guts—was to be clean and to stay clean. That is what she really wanted.

So together we explored strategies to get to clean and sober housing and support systems. There was no more fighting or tension in her body, just a lot of energy focused on solutions. I asked her how it felt when she helped friends in the past, and she acknowledged that she knew how good it felt. So I told her that she was giving somebody a chance to experience just that. She understood.

Later that day, I saw her asking staff for help. She didn't yell, didn't insult them, she just asked for help. I watched from a distance and felt a little smile on my face.

Until the end of her stay with us, she remained calm. She continued to deny that a man had beaten her. She did not want to discuss any part of that story. We knew that the man was known to be a pimp. When she left our unit, I could feel that she was still connected to herself. She was calmer and more at peace. She gave me a real smile; her face was almost back to its normal shape, just a pretty moon face.

While writing my last notes on her chart, I read an additional information sheet from a clinic. It said that she had had 10 pregnancies, six kids, all of them in foster homes, which amounted to quite a record for a woman of only 36 years of age.

The newly lifted weight felt heavy on my shoulders again thinking about her kids. The little light that I saw in her peaceful smile had vanished out of my heart. I tried to stop my mind to create the predictable and stay present with what I saw; a smiling woman ready to stay clean.

Daniela: Frozen

When I got the report about Daniela I was told that she had been there for a little over 10 days and that she was "depressed and delusional." Those were big words that gave her nurse the permission to continue one's paperwork and stay away from the patient.

The first day, as usual, I focused on taking care of her body: "Yes, you have to get up today." I usually give patients the choice of time to shower: "10 or 11 o'clock?" or even "before or after lunch?" This is to give them some control over their highly controlled hospital life. Most medications have sedative effects, so 11 a.m. seems often to be the preferred time to shower. That's the time Daniela chose.

I came back then with the supplies. She showed a bit of resistance but came with me as we had previously agreed. I escorted her to the shower area to unlock the door. I had brought along, as I often do, some hair conditioner from home as a "treat."

Daniela was a small, slightly overweight, Hispanic woman in her mid-20s. I had read in her chart that she was brought by her family because she would not come out of her room and was refusing food, thinking that it was poisoned. I tried to engage her but I didn't get much of a reaction in English or in Spanish, so we focused on small talk like cleaning her room and doing her laundry. Only at the end of the day did I get half a smile from her when I made a comment about her shiny black hair.

On day three, I did the same type of prompting, focusing on body care and encouragement to gain a sense of wellbeing. In one of my attempts to connect with her, I asked her if she could help me understand how a girl like her could go from college to this hospital. She took time to reflect and then slowly began to open up.

She was brought up in the U.S. with family members but her parents stayed in Nicaragua. Now that she was an adult, there was a huge fork in the road and she froze— froze into depression.

On one side was the U.S., where she was now without a home, since her sister, who supported her, had gone back to Nicaragua. She had no way to continue her studies without a home. On the other hand, in Nicaragua she had supportive parents, a place to stay and the possibility of continuing her schooling under a fragile government with the communists coming back into power.

When those two sides were explained, she repeated again that she didn't want to go back to Nicaragua because during her last visit, her mother had held her captive. I listened attentively and I didn't let my mind find a solution that would be *my* solution. I really trusted that in just doing some echoing she would find enough clarity to make a decision on her own.

On the third day, her parents came to visit. They knew that their daughter was sick and had been hospitalized so they had come all the way from Nicaragua. I suggested to the doctor that they have a family meeting, which we did. The father's body posture was peculiar. He was noticeably leaning towards his wife away from the daughter. So we started to talk, or they talked and I translated for the doctor. At one point I asked the daughter's permission to share our previous conversation with her parents. She agreed, so I talked about Daniela's fear of losing her freedom if she went home. Tears welled up in her mother's eyes. She explained that during her daughter's last visit, her own father had died and her niece too. Reaching for a tissue, she explained that she couldn't bear the idea of her daughter leaving Nicaragua.

The mother then turned toward her daughter and started to talk to her as if none of us were in the room.

She gave her reassurance and a commitment that did not require a signature. She explained that the only thing she wanted was to have her daughter back and would give her the freedom and trust she wanted and deserved.

I saw a smile on Daniela's face, a beautiful smile and a shine from her green eyes that I had not seen before. The decision was clear: She would go back to where she had support and could continue her schooling—she would go back to Nicaragua.

I asked her to send me a postcard from Nicaragua.

* * *

Marc: Ex-Navy

Hardly anyone talks to Marc. I guess he is just too "crazy." I must admit, at times, he has the eyes of a madman. This time, his hospitalization had been so long that everybody on the unit was getting used to having him around. His tall thin figure with his grey hair and his goatee were just part of the décor now. Marc didn't initiate conversation and no one wanted to break into his world. Placement seemed insoluble; no board-and-care home was ready to take him. Once in a while, you could see him swearing to himself and then he would go back to his normal silence.

The first day of my weekly three-day shift, I went into what we call the "boutique," a charming name for a small, dark room where we store clothes donated by the hospital staff. There I really think I picked out the perfect outfit for Marc, casual and stylish: a pair of nice jeans and a light-colored linen shirt. After breakfast, I suggested a shower, monitored a shave and gave him the bundle of new clothes. He went to his room to put them on and a little visual miracle happened: Out of a homeless-looking dude came a classy gentleman. The change of appearance made Marc visible to the staff, at least for a while. The visual change was certainly not enough to make him talk or allow others to step into his closed world.

The second day, he actually approached me with a short and to-the-point request: "Can you come and check my room?" Surprised by the request, I agreed without hesitation. I was not sure what to expect—a water leak or a plugged toilet? He held the door open for me to enter and gave me a military salute. Once in, I realized that I was there to inspect the room, so I did. His bed was perfectly made, in a military sense. I guess I could have bounced a coin on it, if I had tried. As if I wore white gloves, I checked for any dust on his empty nightstand. I opened his closet to find his clothes folded with precision. I commented favorably, indicating that I was impressed. He did not move, standing straight as a board, still holding the door open. As I prepared to exit the room, without any facial expression he uttered "and the bathroom" to remind me that I had definitely not completed my inspection. I complied and finished the job, leaving the room with an encouraging nod, exclaiming "Well done."

Later, I saw in his chart that he had been in the Navy. I did not find much more about his history.

This week, Marc was not my patient. As I was walking back to the nurse's station, I saw him sitting on the floor, head down in a big book. I guess I was surprised and pleased to see him with a book and I made a casual comment about it, asking if it was good reading. He mumbled something not very clearly but I heard the words "just too big." So I repeated "So, it is too big?" He nodded and asked me very politely if he could get another book from the library. The library is locked most of the day so patients need to have a staff member escort them to get in. I had a few moments and offered to go with him. In a very short time of searching through the books, he selected a smaller book. "Great," I said. "Let's go." As we were walking out of the room I asked him if I could see his choice. To my surprise it was a book of Jean Giono written in French. A little hesitantly, I said "It is a book written in French." Marc mumbled something about the moon and the sunshine and he appeared convinced that this was the book for him.

Who am I to pretend to know what book is good or not good for someone else?

* * *

Alex: Boxing does not help

I was forewarned that I had an angry male admission called Alex. I walked the long hallway toward the admitting wing of the hospital and as I turned the last corner I saw a young man pacing back and forth in a small room. His head was down and his right fist was repetitively hitting the palm of his left hand.

I stopped at the open door and introduced myself, staying at a safe distance. I explained that I was there to do his admission. I asked if he understood that he was on a three-day legal hold to be evaluated and hopefully helped. With his head still looking at the floor, he answered, "I need help." I felt a sense of relief when I heard that.

We did all the paperwork needed for the admission, during which I asked him 11 pages of questions. He answered most of them, at times with hesitation or maybe some difficulties. He especially had a hard time contracting not to harm others, saying: "If somebody gets into my face, I don't know." That question is essential to answer before anyone can be let into our unit.

During the assessment he shared bits of his tough history. Looking at the floor, he talked about abuse, sexual and physical, from his foster father. Without stopping, as if to continue the tragic saga, he admitted to having sexually abused his little brother. "I did bad things, but I paid for it."

I listened and continued to be present, reminding him that the past cannot be changed, but that today was the first day of a new life that he could choose. He raised his head toward me and gave me half a smile.

As his body was starting to relax a little, he explained that he had a fiancée named Shelly. He was afraid his anger was getting in the way and admitted that he had assaulted her once, adding quickly that she was OK.

My paperwork was done, and he agreed to sign a "no harm contract," so I escorted him to his room. We talked a little longer about what he called "his rage." He talked about the boxing gym he was going to. I explained that to believe that boxing could reduce his impulse control was a myth. Studies had proven that, on the contrary, it could become a learned habit to express anger with his fists. This could increase his rage problem rather than reducing it. We discussed other sports that could release his rage in a more effective way.

I asked him if he thought something could be behind his rage, something that we could call sadness—sadness about so much unfairness, about his stolen childhood and a life so hard to live. He listened and I saw tears in his eyes.

I talked about the power of actions, about choices, and he said he wanted a different life. He talked about his fiancée and the joy to have love in his life. His body relaxed and he visibly went into exhaustion. I left the room to get an extra pillow and he fell asleep like a child. Later that day I checked on him and he was writing a letter to his fiancée. I was looking forward to working two more days with him.

The next day Alex was assigned to another team. I passed him as he was walking the hallways. He gave me a friendly look and a couple of quick shoulder movements like the boxer he was. His fists had resumed the old habit of hitting each other in a rhythmic way.

Carol was the nurse on his team, so I talked to her about his suffering. Under the young angry boxer was an abused child. She listened to me with a powerless expression.

Alex triggered fear in others, he had a criminal record, he was young, healthy and strong, so he was diagnosed with poor impulse control and was started on medications.

    * * *

Logan: More meth

I didn't do Logan's admission. My first encounter with him was in the hallway. He was walking around the unit holding his 5150 paper (a legal hold for three days) and stopping anyone, begging for a few minutes of attention. Logan was about 20 years old and everything about him was average. I stopped a minute to listen to his request and that minute dragged on and on.

"Just wait, wait, read this," he pleaded, holding up the sheet of paper in front of my face. He then explained: "Everything that is written here is wrong. Let me tell you; something is going wrong with my girlfriend, very wrong. And I wish you could just see her and help her."

Hardly taking a breath, he continued: "What good is it going to do for me to be locked up, when the only thing I am asking is for you or anybody else to check on my girlfriend?"

In fact, all this sounded reasonable. Logan, the average guy, was making average sense. If you gave him some attention, he would not let you go. "Let me use the phone, so my girlfriend can come and she can be seen by the doctor." He kept begging and pleading with any staff member who walked by.

He left no room in his speech to ask any questions. When he took a quick breath I interjected: "Yes, I can hear your frustration." Looking at the legal hold that he was still holding in my face, I said: "I cannot change what is written there" and then I added: "Maybe we can help you." He fired back: "I don't need help, my girlfriend needs help." And off he went again.

I finally decided to sit down and listen to him explain the real problem with his girlfriend. Somebody had taken over her body and was inside her mind—that was clear to him. The proof was in her rapid eye movements.

Logan's urine analysis came back positive for amphetamines. He had apparently been taking meth for days. His last dose had been taken that morning at 4 a.m. and was intended for him to stay awake to check on his girlfriend. He had tried to strangle her to take the man out of her head.

***

Victoria: AMA to heaven

Victoria was a young Hispanic woman in her late 30s, short, stocky and quite difficult to describe. The first day I had her on my load of patients, she was moderately pleasant. She would engage in conversation mostly with somatic complaints. She complained mostly of general pain and anxiety. Her high pulse rate tended to confirm anxiety. She was on antipsychotic Zyprexa and a mood stabilizer Luvox. On the chart her diagnosis was given as bipolar. At the same time, the medical orders were to access her every day for auditory hallucinations, not a typical bipolar symptom. Go figure!

The first day, I just tried to establish a bit more trust. I must say she was not an easy patient and had a surfeit of complaints. She even wrote a complaint about not being helped fast enough. I felt that she was at the nurses' station about every half hour or trying to find me on the floor about something new.

The second day I tried to do more active listening and asked her more about her anxiety. She seemed to have gained trust in me and began to share her story, mostly in Spanish with English words here and there.

Of course, she had a history of abuse, which seems to be common for so many mentally ill patients. She also had problems with insomnia, probably related to the abuse. When her son was four years old, she had not slept more than one or two hours per night for almost a whole month. "I went crazy" is how she described her condition when, to avoid him suffering, she considered killing him and herself. Those emotions were coming back as she told me her story of it. I was not asking questions, I was just listening with an open heart. She said that she had thrown her son into a well and then, realizing what she had done, she ran to the neighbor for help getting him out.

Fortunately, he survived, but she was judged incompetent to take care of him and lost custody, including visitation rights. Her sister adopted the child and refused to have anything more to do with her.

She ended the story saying that her physical pain was God punishing her for what she did to the child. I tried with great difficulty to offer some reassurance. I said that she acted when she was sick and that she must have been a good person for the angels to have kept her son alive.

She smiled and then, as if the conversation was over, went back to the reality of the pain and anxiety she was having. One of her common requests was a pregnancy test. Later that day, I saw her in the hallway with a pillow under her T-shirt, walking like a pregnant woman, softly talking to her belly. By the end of the week, I really had a sense that she had gained ease and was less demanding.

The next week the doctor did not feel like she was ready to go but the judge decided she was. I told her that she could come back anytime she wanted to. She replied: "I have to give the outside world a try." She was smiling and I really thought she was the best I had seen her.

She was discharged against medical advice to the care of her family.

    * * *

I was shocked a week later to hear that Victoria hanged herself the night she left the hospital. What happened ?

I rewound the tape over and over. Could I have read her intention when she left the hospital? Any hint of anger, frustration or anything abnormally high that could have indicated that she had made her decision? Nothing, I did not see anything. She had always denied any intention to end her life for religious reasons.

I never got to see the chart again to see if there was anything in my notes or somebody else's notes that I had missed. I came home dragging a heavy heart.

The hospital offered to any staff member interested one or more visits to a therapist. I decided to give it a try and I took my journal and read about Victoria. I had not had the courage to look at it before going to the office. I let the tears roll down my cheeks and told her story.

My chest was tight, my heart crushed within it.

The therapist talked about the limitation of our work, we were doing the best we could and that was limited. This didn't help me at all. Then he said that I could work with a wall around me that would separate me from the mentally ill. That would block the option of feelings. I looked at him with surprise. The other option he said, is to accept feeling what we live. Today I was experiencing grief for somebody I lost and it was a normal emotion. I felt relieved. It was OK for me to cry.

He added as I left that if I was still crying after two weeks to come back and we would explore how that grieving was possibly related to a loss in my own life. I did not feel the need to go back.

I felt lighter accepting my feelings with tender love.

* * *

Susanna: No place like home

It was strange that Susanna was the one who remained in my head this week. I didn't even want to write a daily report on her. I traded her chart with Elizabeth, my psych tech. Elizabeth and I had shared the same 11 patients for three days, so switching the charts at the end of our third day was a normal team trade.

I had more high-profile patients—like Takuya, a young Japanese man who was brought by the police after he was found walking on the hillside yelling about the Japanese mafia, dressed only in camouflage duct tape all over his body. I also had an older Laotian man who, after losing his business and the dignity that comes with it, was streaking in front of his house, maybe an act of desperation. But still, Susanna was the one that stuck in my head.

Susanna was a pretty, tall and thin 59-year-old woman with a moonlike face and big thick glasses. She appeared casually dressed. Looking at her skin and her hair I was guessing maybe the possibility of poor health.

When the psychiatrist interviewed her, she appeared to have a very concrete way of thinking. She was clearly anxious and preoccupied about the discharge plans. "You know how it is," she explained. "There's no place like home. It feels good to be home." Then she would talk about the dogs. How much she missed the dogs. "Yeah, they're just like my kids, you know." This all seems to make sense.

Acording to the social worker's notes, she was living in conditions that were declared "unsafe." I read that the house was full of fleas. She herself appeared neat so I felt compassion for the lady who had a problem with fleas and had no apparent flamboyant mental disorder.

Later that day the social worker gave me a little more information. Suzanna had a citation for animal abuse as her dogs were undernourished and had sores and fleas. Then we saw a couple of pictures of her house. It was so difficult to comprehend. The house was completely full of trash. Actually, more trash inside than outside. The picture of the kitchen showed a narrow path between mountains of trash. My jaw fell open.

During a later interview we showed her the pictures of what she was calling "home." She looked at them and asked: "If I get someone to help me to clean the house, can I go home?" Then she added, "You know how days go. You just get busy, I have to walk the dogs and then I am too tired to clean."

From making concrete sense to a vision of something which is beyond sense and from trying to understand to not understanding—I ended up being the one confused that day.

* * *

Martin: You slaughter a cow

I am not sure when I first saw Martin. It must have been on my morning rounds, when I go room to room to make sure everybody is alive. It is my first task and it is the way I start my day! A lot of my patients come into the hospital after an overdose, often in a suicide attempt. They have their stomach charcoaled but sometimes the blood toxicity continues to rise, putting them at risk of going into a coma. So I am careful and at 7:30 a.m. I do my rounds and expect an answer or a moan to my morning greetings.

I am guessing Martin was too sleepy to make an impact on me when I introduced myself that morning.

Martin was a 22-year-old, very fit Latino young man. He had a handsome face, buzzed hair and the parts of his body showing were covered with tattoos. During the first long conversation we had, I remember noticing that he could not meet my eyes. He would almost raise his head to face me and then, as if it was a task too hard to accomplish, he would lower his head down. He would then look at the door or his bed. Our conversation at first was very concrete. I noticed quickly that he could share his feelings with ease. He had the vocabulary of a well-read person and was interested in discussing ideas, and he challenged my questions. He told me right away that anger was his problem: "I wake up angry, that is who I am."

I asked him: "Is this who you want to be?" He gave me a puzzled look. He seemed to have adopted the identity of "I am angry" and did not question it.

Anger is a subject that fascinates me. It has the power to destroy or to give birth to something new.

After spending more than 10 years facilitating "anger management classes" I am really convinced that managing or controlling anger is just the wrong approach. I am more interested in seeing anger as a package that has a hidden longing inside.

In a later conversation with Martin, he started to share bits and pieces of his life. I did not ask questions, I just remained present.

At age 12, he witnessed his mother shooting and killing his father. He explained that he tried hard to stop the fight by getting the gun, but failed. His shoulders still seemed heavy as he told the story. When the police arrived he had the gun his mother used in his hand, wanting to shoot his mother. Can this be called a childhood? His mother, he explained, got charged with manslaughter and was sentenced to six years in jail. Why "slaughter," he asked with his teeth clenched. "You slaughter a cow. My father was not a cow."

He talked about the multiple foster homes in which he had grown up. He seemed detached talking about a life he did not choose. When he turned 18 he went back "home" to his grandma and sister. "They are scared of me," he explained. "That is why I am here."

Martin knew a lot about anger. He mentioned with a slight shift in his voice that he was not satisfied with his life. Without much guidance on my part he was able to connect with the sadness that was underneath his anger. We stayed present with that observation.

I asked him if he had anything that brought joy to his life. It was hard for him to find any. When I brought up short-term satisfaction, he lit up and knew what I was talking about. The stealing, the intimidating, the yelling—that is what he knew. Long-term satisfaction, the real joy, he was not sure of. He was searching but was not convinced.

I suggested that long-term satisfaction, also called happiness, can be found. He smiled, giving me the "oh yeah" with doubts, but he was willing to continue exploring. We talked about choices, about school, about things we cannot change. Then he mentioned a dream he had, of one day becoming a phlebotomist, and with a shoulder shrug he dismissed the idea like it was a joke.

When he was called to see the psychiatrist, Dr. L, the interview lasted about three minutes. She asked that the case to be transferred to a male doctor. I guess he seemed too intimidating for her. I asked Martin: "What happened with the doctor?" He answered: "She's not happy." He raised his face toward mine and our eyes met in comfortable trust. He gave me a sweet smile, letting me see two broken front teeth.

I got busy that day and didn't get a chance to talk more with him. On Sunday, the end of my week at the hospital, I wrote on top of a page "I will be a phlebotomist" and in slightly smaller print I wrote "What can I do today to bring long satisfaction to my life?" I gave him the page folded in half. He read it and gave me the biggest smile. "I never thought of it like this, I get it," and we shook hands.

　　　* * *

Paul: Red light

Paul spends most of his day staring at the red EXIT
sign above our double doors. From morning to night those
doors, leading to our community room, are propped open.
It is a very high-traffic zone on our unit, so patients and
staff go around him, as if he was a pole in a slalom race.
After passing by him a few times, I just had to ask gently,
"What are you looking at?" Without hesitation he said,
"I'm waiting for it to turn green." I got the sense that he
was on a mission and I certainly did not want to interrupt
him.

Later that day, looking at his chart, I found out that
this so-called mentally ill person had served in Vietnam. He
had kept a sense of diligence in his mission.

* * *

Derek: Sad Johnny Depp

Derek was 27 years old but looked like he was barely 21. The staff on the unit had a clear judgment about him. He was a "repeat," a "manipulator" and the worst label of all, a "sociopath." The advice given to me that day was "don't believe anything he says."

He looked like a movie character that Johnny Depp would play, dressed in black, face really pale, often wearing dark makeup around his eyes and a long black coat flapping on the back of his legs.

I had seen him many times on our unit and this time he was not assigned to my load of patients. Around noon I heard that he had cut himself "again" and had to be taken to the emergency room for sutures. I noticed that his nurse was swamped with a difficult admission, so I offered to take him. Before we left, the doctor put on a temporary dressing and I took Derek in a wheelchair to the emergency room.

While we were waiting he confided in me that he had hidden a razor blade in his sock at the time of his admission. He told me "I just wanted to finish the job I started." The day of his admission Derek had needed 20 stitches on his wrists for self-inflicted cuts.

"Whoa," the doctor exclaimed, when she saw how deep the cuts were after removing the temporary dressing. She asked Derek to hold still and she left to get a suture kit. Walking by me she mumbled "You've got to take the razors away from those guys." "Thanks for the advice!" I thought to myself.

I got a look at Derek's wound while she was gone and told him how much it hurt me to see the deep cuts in him. The doctor came back and put in eight sutures. Derek showed no sign of pain.

When we got back on the unit he mumbled "nobody takes me seriously." Derek was put on a one-to-one.

The next day while I was changing his dressing I realized how deep his depression was. I tried to help buoy him up by talking about his two kids. He said that for a year and a half he had not seen his six- and two-year-old girls.

Having other patients to see, I asked him to write about his goals and gave him paper and a pencil.

Later that day, I took him to see the psychiatrist and sat down with him during the session. I had noticed that his thinking was concrete and that the psychiatrist had to rephrase questions to him several times for him to understand. The psychiatrist asked him what was going on in his head when he went to his grandmother's grave and slashed both his wrists. He could not explain, or refused to answer.

The following day while changing his dressing, Derek asked me how long the scars were going to be visible. I thought his concern was a good sign of him looking into the future. He said a few words about his stolen childhood, about his abusive mother and his fond memories of his grandmother who raised him.

When I asked him to talk about his daughters, he was vague and kept repeating "I have lost all my loved ones." He didn't know where his kids were and he denied having any restraining order against him.

I found out at the end of the shift that most of the information he gave me was true. However, he "forgot" to tell me that he physically abused his wife and that she had left him. The older daughter, while in custody of her mother, was placed under Child Protective Services for neglect. The mother was under 18 when she had her.

It was easy to judge him simply because he was a "repeat." Does he need to kill himself to be taken seriously?

* * *

Ron: Manic with a plan

This was the first hospitalization for this 38-year-old man. I don't like labels but I must say that Ron looked like a textbook bipolar case.

At breakfast time, a couple of staff members asked me: "What do you want to do with Ron?" as he was already loud and intrusive. What they were really asking me was: "Do something to control Ron."

It had been stated in a report that he had been in seclusion the first day for "threatening behavior" and I had to care for the rug burn he suffered during the takedown.

I approached him and asked if we could talk a little. He responded: "Can we walk and talk?" So we walked and talked, or *we* walked and *he* talked. There was not much space for me to say anything. He talked about the multiple corporations he was running and the websites he was designing. He really could talk.

To be sure that I got all his information he invited me to see his room. There were papers all over the floor and covering his bed. He started to explain the new design for the website that he just created and he showed me words I could not read, written with toothpaste on his locker.

I thanked him for sharing his story and I explained that some order in his room would make it easier for me to understand him. He agreed. His speech was still pressured but he started to pick up papers from the floor. Continuing talking and pointing to the smoke detectors in the ceiling he explained that his information was already "all over Eyewitness News."

He signed a consent form to be started on Depakote, which is commonly used to relieve the symptoms of bipolar disorder, and was given his first dose.

After a good night's sleep he was a different man. At least I no longer had the staff on my back about him. His speech was still continuous but less pressured and intense, and less intrusive. Each time he saw me he asked if we could walk and talk. He didn't leave me much room to explain the condition of bipolar disorder.

On his third day, when his legal hold was up, he asked to be released. He said that he felt like a million bucks and was ready.

I explained that the doctor had written the 5250 papers, allowing us to hold him until the next court day, which was two days away. I read him the doctor's reasons to keep him longer, being "continuation of treatment to increase stabilization." I told him what the court would look for on Thursday. He was able to sit and listen.

He said he was in a hurry to go home to file for a divorce, because he had caught his wife cheating, and added that she was the cause of this hospitalization.

I tried to explain that it was thanks to his wife that he got treated here and felt so much better. He agreed for a second and continued to talk about their $600,000 home, the equity he had in the house and all the other investments he had in his Dow Jones account.

At the end of my three days with him, as I was doing my last round, Ron was calmly sitting watching TV. I told him that it was the end of my shift. He was very thankful for my help and explained that he felt ready for the court on Tuesday. He reassured me that he would be discharged by the court and added "but I will be back to teach an art program here to help patients to express themselves through art and music."

I smiled.   * * *

Isaiah: Out of prison

I woke up Isaiah to tell him that breakfast was being served in the community room. He seemed disinterested, so I added that we were having French toast that morning. A few minutes later he appeared to pick up his breakfast tray.

When the breakfast was over with all the trays picked up, he remained seated at his table. I moved closer to him and he asked politely in an English accent if he could go back to his room.

My quick assumption was that this 26-year-old muscular man was probably just out of prison. I don't like assumptions but that is where my brain took me. He was used to being told where to go, what to do and to ask permission before doing anything. I gently explained our schedule and began asking whether he knew why he was with us. Being a man of few words, his first response was "I don't belong here" followed by "I don't know why I'm here."

I asked him if he had read his copy of the 5150, explaining that all our patients were given a copy upon admission. He denied having one, or just could not find it, so I went to the nurse's station and made a copy to hand to him. I explained that he didn't have to agree with the content and that our job was to prove that he was safe to return to society. It was clear that I would get nowhere by asking questions since he was defensive and closed. So I backed off for a while.

Staff members had commented to me that he was strong and muscular and looked "guarded and paranoid." His legal hold said that he had been hospitalized six months before for the same reason of "threatening someone with a knife." I checked the records and found no sign of him being hospitalized. I checked with the

Admission and Referral unit in case they had a file on him, but there were no records of a previous hospitalization or even an evaluation.

To me that meant that at least one element of this 5150 wasn't true. I waited to tell him and went back to casual conversation about schedules, showering and so forth in an attempt to build trust and I made some progress.

He said he was living alone. He knew nothing about a knife and said that "all this was a lie." I asked him if we could talk to anyone who could confirm that it was safe to let him go home. He said to talk to his sister. I was relieved to have someone from the outside to talk to. He signed a consent form and I obtained his sister's information.

His sister seemed relieved to talk to somebody about Isaiah. She explained that her brother was released from prison just a month before. The sister did not tell me why he spent three years in prison. That was the past. She shared her concerns about his drug use and his depression. He had broken his parole by being under the influence of meth. She thought that he had not dealt with his mother's passing while he was in prison. When he got out he learned that his father had moved back to Mexico to start a new family. I thanked her for helping me to understand her brother.

I was glad I got all this information. It gave me a better understanding of a man who in prison had learned not to share his feelings with anyone and had deep reasons to be depressed.

I gave all this information to the doctor, who listened in a slightly distracted manner and wrote down "Paranoid Personality Disorder" as a diagnosis.

I received a later phone call from his sister, who said that two gay women were living in her father's house when Isaiah went home. Apparently one of them had a brief love affair with the "pretty boy out of jail," which did not go well with her partner. Isaiah's sister asked the two women to move out and they became very angry. I wondered if the angry woman made up the knife story to get rid of him. I will probably never know.

Maybe that 5150 was bogus after all. It is possible that Isaiah was right. It is possible that he didn't belong with us.

I was glad that I had a more complete picture, but at the end he was still held for the three days required by the hold. When I left after my days with him, he had become more talkative and less guarded.

I do love those opening buds.

* * *

Liz: From nurse to patient

On December 4, I was assigned to the Admission and Referral Unit (the old Crisis Team).

After each of the several rotations I had done there, I had written a long page under the title of "my safety concerns about this unit." Each time I gave it to my supervisor, she referred it to her supervisor, who probably referred it up the organizational chain.

On that day, two nurses and I were covering the unit without a security guard on duty or other health technicians present to be with us.

We were working on the assessment of people brought in by the police or by their families. Our only safety resource was to call a "Code Grey," knowing that it would take minutes for help to reach us.

I had arrived early as usual to get prepared for my shift when a woman brought in her brother to be assessed. She said that she couldn't have him in her house any longer. She had children and they were afraid of him.

I did my usual preliminary assessment, beginning with a visual. He was well groomed, calm and cooperative. He followed me into the hospital and sat down in the assessment room. I offered him food and drink since it was breakfast time, which he accepted.

My colleagues checked his records and found that he was a meth user. He seemed difficult to read, and before I started my interview I asked my colleague to watch my back since I was uncertain about him.

Seconds later, without showing any sign of anger and without saying a word, the young man stood up. His fists were tightly clenched and his eyes showed determination.

I tried to get through to him, saying, "We are here to help you. We are only here to help," as I swiftly backed up toward the safety of the nurses' station.

My colleague, taking in the scene from behind the glass, called a "Code Grey" and opened the door for me to get away from him. We struggled to close the door, but he was too strong for us.

One massive blow with a tight fist hit my colleague on the temple. The blow was so hard that she was propelled onto the floor with blood gushing from her. She was unconscious and remained on the floor in a pool of blood until she was rescued. The second nurse was stuck in her cubby and yelling, then suddenly fell silent. He then pursued me as I tried to escape. He tackled me and proceeded to bash my head against the floor until my co-workers arrived to save me.

Those horrible moments flashed through my mind again and again for months on end. I kept thinking, "If only we had been able to secure the door into the nursing station." I wallowed in the "what ifs," which are classical signs of post-traumatic stress disorder (PTSD).

From being a nurse, I had now become a patient.

In one day, my life had been transformed. The trauma had injured my brain. I had difficulty getting out of the house alone or even going to the store without having debilitating panic attacks. My logical brain had been hijacked. I was clearly not able to work, my nursing income was gone and my self image was shattered. I was lost.

And what kind of nurse was I for myself? I had judgments, opinions and advice—just what I stayed away from with all my patients. I would go from "Get over it, you did not go to Iraq" to "It was not that bad, we all came out alive" to " You have failed, you have completely failed." I was blaming myself over and over.

I could not find blame or anger inside me against that young man who was so determined to hurt nurses. I never had a chance to gain an understanding of his determination.

I did feel some anger towards the hospital for not protecting my colleagues and me, but it is not easy to hold anger against an institution so it changed into sadness. I must say that now, after the "accident," they got the security guards we asked for. Good for them.

With the support of my sweet family and friends I started to heal. I took some time to observe my body during my panic attacks that I called my waves of fear. I stopped resisting them and they became more gentle.

It took me more than two years to understand that the same deep compassionate listening that I was giving to my patients, I could give to myself. I accepted my sadness without judgment, without trying to fix it. My brain and my heart started to heal and joy slowly reappeared in my life.

To gently care for myself was my most difficult nursing task and my silver lining.

* * *